D1612372

THE VICTORIA HISTORY
OF THE
COUNTIES OF ENGLAND

———

A HISTORY OF
CAMBRIDGESHIRE
AND
THE ISLE OF ELY
VOLUME VII

THE VICTORIA HISTORY
OF THE
COUNTIES OF ENGLAND

EDITED BY C. R. ELRINGTON

THE UNIVERSITY OF LONDON

INSTITUTE OF

HISTORICAL RESEARCH

Oxford University Press

OXFORD   LONDON   GLASGOW
NEW YORK   TORONTO   MELBOURNE   WELLINGTON
KUALA LUMPUR   SINGAPORE   JAKARTA   HONG KONG   TOKYO
DELHI   BOMBAY   CALCUTTA   MADRAS   KARACHI
IBADAN   NAIROBI   DAR ES SALAAM   CAPE TOWN

© *University of London 1978*

ISBN 0 19 722748 1

Printed in Great Britain
at the University Press, Oxford
by Vivian Ridler
Printer to the University

INSCRIBED TO THE

MEMORY OF HER LATE MAJESTY

QUEEN VICTORIA

WHO GRACIOUSLY GAVE THE TITLE TO

AND ACCEPTED THE DEDICATION

OF THIS HISTORY

BRONZE BUST OF THE EMPEROR COMMODUS, FROM BULLOCK'S HASTE ($\frac{1}{1}$). [pp. 80–1]

A HISTORY OF THE COUNTY OF

CAMBRIDGE

AND

THE ISLE OF ELY

ROMAN CAMBRIDGESHIRE

EDITED BY J. J. WILKES AND C. R. ELRINGTON

VOLUME VII

PUBLISHED FOR

THE INSTITUTE OF HISTORICAL RESEARCH

BY

OXFORD UNIVERSITY PRESS

1978

Distributed by Oxford University Press until 1 January 1981
thereafter by Dawsons of Pall Mall

CONTENTS OF VOLUME SEVEN

LIST OF ILLUSTRATIONS

For permission to reproduce photographs of objects in their possession thanks are offered to the trustees of the British Museum, the Ashmolean Museum, Oxford, and especially the Cambridge Museum of Archaeology and Ethnology; for permission to reproduce their copyright photographs, to Mr. T. F. C. Blagg, the Warburg Institute, and especially to the Committee for Aerial Photography, University of Cambridge. Where it is not otherwise stated, photographs were supplied by the Cambridge Museum of Archaeology and Ethnology.

LIST OF ILLUSTRATIONS

LIST OF MAPS AND OTHER ILLUSTRATIONS
IN THE TEXT

The maps and diagrams were drawn by K. J. Wass from drafts prepared by D. M. Browne and, for the map of Cambridge, J. A. Alexander. The maps are based on the Ordnance Survey with the sanction of the Controller of H.M. Stationery Office, Crown Copyright reserved. The inscriptions on milestones are reproduced by kind permission of the Clarendon Press and Mr. Wright.

EDITORIAL NOTE

THE account of Roman Cambridgeshire now published completes the general articles planned for the county. The structure and aims of the series as a whole are outlined in the *General Introduction* to the *History* (1970). The names of counties by which places outside Cambridgeshire are identified in the text below are those of the counties as existing on 31 March 1974.

A few words on the compilation of the volume may be helpful. In 1974 Professor Wilkes agreed to write the article on Roman Cambridgeshire, but shortly afterwards learned that Mr. Browne, who had been engaged for some time on a doctoral thesis about the Roman remains of the Cambridge region, had made a thorough survey of the evidence. It was therefore agreed that Mr. Browne should write the article under the editorial control of Professor Wilkes. While the scheme of the article was devised jointly by Professor Wilkes and Mr. Browne, the presentation of the evidence and the conclusions drawn from it are essentially Mr. Browne's; much of the actual wording belongs to Professor Wilkes, whose contribution included shortening the first, fuller draft of the article. The work aims to take into account material published up to 1976.

The division of Cambridgeshire between the fenland in the north and the Cambridge region in the south is made the sharper for the historian of the Roman period by the work of his predecessors. For southern Cambridgeshire Sir Cyril Fox's *The Cambridge Region*, first published in 1924 and reissued with an appendix in 1948, provides the indispensable starting point, while for the northern part of the county the Royal Geographical Society's *The Fenland in Roman Times*, edited by C. W. Phillips (1970), has made it relatively easy to rehearse the evidence afforded by the Cambridgeshire fenland. Just as neither work covers the whole county, neither confines itself to Cambridgeshire: the Fenland Research Committee took in the whole fenland, and the Cambridge region treated by Fox, bounded on the north by an arbitrary line on the latitude of Ely, included the corner of Huntingdonshire around Godmanchester, the two projections of Bedfordshire into west Cambridgeshire, and the peninsula of Suffolk at Newmarket. The present volume is greatly indebted to both works, whose differences of approach and archaeological method it naturally reflects.

The help of many people and institutions in the compilation of the volume is gratefully acknowledged. For the most part it is recorded in appropriate places below, but special mention must here be made of Miss Joan Liversidge and her colleagues at the Cambridge Museum of Archaeology and Ethnology, of Dr. J. A. Alexander and his colleagues working under the aegis of the Cambridge Board of Extra-Mural Studies and the London Department of Extra-Mural Studies, of Professor A. L. F. Rivet, and of Professor J. K. St. Joseph. For help of a different sort thanks are offered to the British Academy, which made a generous grant towards the costs of travelling, typing, and preparing the maps and other illustrations.

NOTE ON ABBREVIATIONS

Among the abbreviations and short titles more frequently used the following may require elucidation:

Alexander, Excavation Rep.
J. A. Alexander, D. Trump, R. Hull, R. Farrar, and (for 1969) I. Kinnis, 'Excavations in Cambridge, 1964–7', 'Arbury Road, Cambridge, 1968', and 'Excavations in Cambridge, 1969', being reports issued by the Board of Extra-Mural Studies, Cambridge, and the Department of Extra-Mural Studies, London, 1967, 1968, and 1969

Antiq. Jnl.
Society of Antiquaries of London, *The Antiquaries Journal*

Arch. Jnl.
Royal Archaeological Institute, *Archaeological Journal*

B.A.R.
British Archaeological Reports

Babington, *Ancient Cambs.*
C. C. Babington, *Ancient Cambridgeshire* (2nd edn. 1883, C.A.S. 8vo ser. xx)

Britannia
Britannia: A Journal of Romano-British and Kindred Studies

C.A.S. *Rep.*
Cambridge Antiquarian Society, Annual *Report*. The reports numbered 11–48 (for 1851–88) were published under a cover bearing the titles *Report* and *Communications*, and in many libraries the two are bound together, cf. below, *Proc. C.A.S.*

Camb. Mus.
Cambridge Museum of Archaeology and Ethnology

Fox, *Arch. Camb. Region*
C. F. Fox, *Archaeology of the Cambridge Region* (1923, reissued with a new appendix 1948)

J.R.S.
Journal of Roman Studies

Jnl. Brit. Arch. Assoc.
Journal of the British Archaeological Association

Margary, *Roads*
I. D. Margary, *Roman Roads in Britain* (3rd edn. 1973)

Num. Chron.
Numismatic Chronicle

P. N. Cambs. (E.P.N.S.)
P. H. Reany, *The Place-Names of Cambridgeshire and the Isle of Ely* (English Place-Name Society, vol. xix, 1943)

Proc. C.A.S.
Proceedings of the Cambridge Antiquarian Society, including vols. i–vi which are entitled *Communications*. The *Communications* have three distinct sequences of numbers, of volumes, of separate yearly issues, and of individual contributions. Vols. vii–xvii (the first eleven to be entitled *Proceedings*) are also numbered as New Series i–xi. Only the volume-numbers of the continuous series are cited below. *Reports* numbered 11–19 form part of vol. i, 20–4 of vol. ii, 37–40 of vol. iv, 41–4 of vol. v, 45–8 of vol. vi.

R.C.H.M.
Royal Commission on Historical Monuments (England)

Roman Fenland
The Fenland in Roman Times, edited by C. W. Phillips for the Royal Geographical Society (1970)

ROMAN CAMBRIDGESHIRE

HISTORICAL SURVEY

CAMBRIDGESHIRE has no history in the Roman period, that is, in the sense that no event in the recorded history of Roman Britain can be associated with any place, either known or unknown, that lay within the county. The initial conquest in A.D. 43, the disarming of south-east Britain and imposition of civil rule, and the rebellion of Icenian Boudicca and the Trinovantes in A.D. 61, all presumably had some direct impact on the area, as did the later events recorded during the disintegration of Roman authority in the late 4th century and early 5th. Moreover neither for the earlier nor for the later of these periods does the archaeological record contribute more than the most meagre quantity of evidence. For the remainder of the Roman period in between the county lay well within the civil part of Roman Britannia, quite removed from direct contact with events in the military history of the northern frontier. Administratively it belonged probably to the territories of two 'cities' (*civitates*), organized by the Romans among the British population of the area, Verulamium of the Catuvellauni and Venta (Caister St. Edmund, Norf.) of the Iceni.

In the late summer of A.D. 43 a substantial part of south-east Britain was formally surrendered to Rome at a ceremony in the presence of the victorious Roman emperor Claudius (A.D. 41–54) at Camulodunum (Colchester), capital of the former British ruler Cunobelinus (d. *c.* A.D. 40). The conquest, achieved by military victories of the consular general Aulus Plautius (consul A.D. 29), had been contrived largely for the political benefit of a conspicuously unmilitary emperor forced upon an unwilling Senate by the praetorian guard after the assassination of his nephew Gaius (Caligula) during the luncheon interval at the Palatine Games on 24 January A.D. 41. The British surrender placed Cunobelinus' kingdom, along with those of other rulers who surrendered at the same time, 'under the jurisdiction of the Roman people' (*sub dicione populi Romani*). Such surrender (*deditio*) could result in annexation and direct Roman rule, as happened with the Trinovantes, among whom Legio xx was stationed at Camulodunum, or to the retention of the native ruler as a Roman client, as perhaps Prasutagus of the Iceni, whose death after a long and successful reign was followed by the rebellion of his deposed widow Boudicca. Elsewhere an imperial favourite from the British or Gallic nobility could be set up with a principality, as with Ti. Claudius Cogidubnus recorded as 'king and legate of the emperor' at Noviomagus (Chichester).[1]

What little evidence there is suggests that most of Cambridgeshire belonged to the Catuvellauni, a people who had once been part of the kingdom of Cunobelinus, except for a portion of the northern and eastern fenlands that may have belonged to the Iceni. A burial from Snailwell has been recognized as of a 'Catuvellaunian type', while the distribution of Icenian coin hoards has led to the suggestion that the boundary between the two peoples ran along the rivers Lark and Kennett.[2]

[1] See S. S. Frere, *Britannia* (2nd edn. 1974), 78–85.

[2] The political geography of southern Britannia is surveyed by A. L. F. Rivet, *Town and Country in Roman Britain* (2nd edn. 1964), 131–79. For the northern boundary of the Trinovantes, see *V.C.H. Essex*, iii. 5, 16. For the Snailwell burial, see T. C. Lethbridge, in *Proc. C.A.S.* xlvii (1954), 25–37. A boundary between Catuvellauni and Iceni along the Lark and Kennett is suggested by D. F. Allen, in *Britannia*, i (1970), 4.

Although there is no evidence that local submission to Roman authority was other than orderly, it was presumably marked by the presence, in the early stages at least, of the Roman army, both legions and auxiliaries. The Ermine Street was in origin a military road, marking probably the line of the northward advance of Legio IX Hispana and its auxiliaries. To the same period belong the military bases at Cambridge and at Godmanchester, where that road crosses the river Ouse just beyond the county boundary. No Roman 'frontier' appears to have existed in the area, and the absence of early Roman military objects from within the county perhaps indicates the essentially transient character of any Roman military occupation. The settlement of A.D. 43 appears to have left the Iceni in the condition of a Roman client state under native rule, an authority which had once made formal surrender but had been reconstituted and allowed to continue at the imperial pleasure. Coins of the Iceni struck at the period record the rule of one Antedios, although their variety suggests that they were issued independently by different groups among the people. Certainly Prasutagus' name is absent.[3]

No record survives of the course of events during the later years of A. Plautius' governorship (A.D. 43–7) but when the narrative of Tacitus resumes in A.D. 47 his successor P. Ostorius Scapula was faced with a revival of British royal power under Caratacus, the surviving son of Cunobelinus. Although the threat came from among the Silures and Ordovices in the west, Ostorius judged it prudent to underline Roman authority in the new province south of the Trent–Severn line. The strict application of the Roman public law (*lex Iulia de vi publica*) demanded universal disarmament of the native population. When the measure was applied also to the Iceni they, along with other peoples, objected and the Roman army had to be sent in to crush resistance. An association of the native earthwork with an Icenian coin hoard at Stonea Camp led to a suggestion that the earthwork might have been the site of an engagement during those operations, but the hoard now appears to be of a later date.[4]

A consequence of Roman intervention may have been the installation of the pro-Roman Prasutagus as ruler of the Iceni. The centre of his power may have lain east of the fenlands in the Breckland. The coins of his regime are likely to be those with the legend ECEN or ECE. While Ostorius' victory was achieved by auxiliaries, the legions were probably in readiness close by, Legio IX on the west or north-west and Legio XX at Camulodunum. When the latter was moved to the Gloucester area a colony of Roman veterans was imposed upon the Trinovantes, settlers who were obligated to take up arms again under the command of their civic magistrates in time of emergency.[5]

In or shortly before A.D. 61 Prasutagus of the Iceni died. The successful reign of this Roman client may have encouraged local hopes that the dynasty might be retained in power, even though the deceased ruler had named the emperor as his coheir, as protocol demanded. When the agents of the Roman finance officer in Britain (*procurator Augusti*) Decianus Catus appeared on the scene those hopes were dashed and the queen Boudicca rebelled. The Trinovantes who had suffered from the Roman colonists in their midst joined her and sacked the colony at Camulodunum with relish. The Roman governor of the province, C. Suetonius Paulinus, had led his army far away to capture the famous shrine of the Druids on the island Mona (Anglesey) largely in an attempt to match his

[3] Allen, in *Britannia*, i. 14.

[4] The governorship of Scapula is described by Tacitus, *Ann.* xii. 31–40; cf. Frere, *Britannia*, 92–9. For Stonea Camp see the aerial photograph in *Roman Fenland*, plate 1b with p. 218. On the coin hoard, G. Fowler, in *Proc. C.A.S.* xliii (1950), 16; cf. Allen, in *Britannia*, i. 16–18;

Frere, *Britannia*, 93.

[5] For Icenian coinage, Allen, in *Britannia*, i. 15–16. The relationship between fortress and *colonia* at Colchester has recently been demonstrated on the ground: see *Britannia*, v (1974), 439–42 with figs. 13–14 (P. Crummy).

rival Corbulo, Roman commander in the east, in public esteem. Returning to the south-east Suetonius could not save London or the municipium of the Catuvellauni at Verulamium and even his final victory over the rebels was for a time threatened by the wilful disobedience of the acting commander of one of his four legions. Suetonius felt cheated of his glory and began to take vengeance on the province. The new procurator, C. Julius Classicianus, advised Rome that a new governor should be sent to pursue a more conciliatory policy. Less concerned about military glory in Britain than Claudius and more mindful of the well-being of the province in the longer term, Nero's ministers took the advice and Suetonius was recalled after a barely decent interval.[6]

Lying at the heart of the area affected by the rebellion, adjacent to the Iceni, Trinovantes, and Catuvellauni, the people then dwelling within the county saw both the rebellion and the equally unpleasant aftermath, even though except for the probable fort at Cambridge no material remains have been discovered to corroborate the fact. Just across the county boundary the military base at Great Chesterford (Essex) may also have been occupied at the time. The Icenian coin hoards from Joist Fen in Waterbeach, Wimblington, and March, may have been buried when Roman reprisals were taking place.[7] It now seems likely that they, and similar Icenian hoards from outside the county, were deposited during the Boudiccan troubles. There are now no grounds to support an older notion that the fenlands were colonized by defeated Iceni in the years following the rebellion. As is described later, the lack of settlement in the fenlands so noticeable in Iron Age times persisted for some decades after the Roman conquest, and the large-scale Roman expansion of settlement in the area is now seen to begin only in the early 2nd century. The consequences of the rebellion for the Roman administration of the area are unknown. It may be that the aggrieved Catuvellauni were awarded new territories in the fenlands reaching to the Wash, although such constructions are perhaps too hypothetical.[8]

Little or nothing is known of how the events of the 2nd, 3rd, 4th, and early 5th centuries impinged on Cambridgeshire. As the survey of Roman settlement shows, the 2nd century was a time of expansion and material prosperity, especially in the fenlands which probably belonged to an imperial estate, falling back quite sharply in the mid 3rd century. Some recovery is evident in the 4th century, although it never reached the earlier levels of the 2nd. The late 4th is likely to have been troubled but Roman life and the accompanying social order, now including Christianity, may have continued in some places well into the 5th.

In the late 2nd century the provincial governor D. Clodius Albinus was defeated in A.D. 197 by his rival claimant for the imperial throne Septimius Severus. Confiscations of property belonging to supporters of Albinus in the province may have involved some estates in the area, leading to an increase in the possibly already substantial imperial holdings. In the reign of Severus (193–211) Britannia was divided into two provinces, Superior (which included the legionary bases at Caerleon and Chester) ruled from the old provincial capital London, and Inferior with its capital at York and including also the colony at Lincoln. If, as is conceivable, the boundary between the two provinces south of Lincoln ran along the Fen Causeway then part of the county was included in Britannia Inferior, although most of it remained in Superior.[9]

Coin hoards reflect the increasing insecurity of the late 3rd century. The separatist

---

[6] For a detailed account see D. R. Dudley and G. Webster, *Rebellion of Boudicca* (1962).

[7] Allen, in *Britannia*, i. 18. On the base at Great Chesterford see W. Rodwell, in *Britannia*, iii (1972), 292–3.

[8] P. Salway, in *Roman Fenland*, 7–9. Cf. Silvia J. Hallam, ibid. 74 (on Catuvellauni): 'initial settlers came

from the vigorous Belgic tribe which had pushed its sphere of influence up through the East Midlands round the western edge of the Fen basin.'

[9] Salway, in *Roman Fenland*, 15–16; and for the Fen Causeway as a possible provincial boundary, ibid. 20 n. 26.

regime of the Gallic Empire under Postumus and his successors (258–73) and the more restricted British-based regime of Carausius and Allectus (286–96) are represented in the area only by the circulation of their coinages. The latter power was suppressed by Constantius I Chlorus, whose restoration of the central authority in Britain is attested by a number of milestones, including one, possibly two, set up on the Cambridge–Godmanchester road when his son Constantine I had succeeded him (A.D. 306–7).

Like the rest of the Roman world the revived Britain of the 4th century had to be defended against new and more dangerous enemies who came by land and sea. The walling of Cambridge c. 340 may indicate a military presence, perhaps a detachment associated with the system of coastal defence known as the Saxon Shore. Its commander was killed, and the general of the provincial army besieged or captured, in the invasions of 367. By then East Anglia may have begun to be settled by the English, following their compatriots who came earlier to serve Rome as *foederati*. The ineffectiveness of the central government led to local usurpations of the imperial authority, if not unilateral British independence. Formal authority may have been conceded to the British cities by a letter from the emperor Honorius in 410 when, according to Procopius, Britain passed under the rule of usurpers.[10]

Place-Names

Two places and a river recorded in ancient written sources have been identified within the county, with varying degrees of certainty.

1. Duroliponte (Cambridge)

Part of the fifth Iter listed for the province of Britain in the Antonine Itinerary runs as follows:[11]

Colonia	m(ilia) p(assuum) xxiiii
Villa Faustini	m. p. xxxv
Icinos	m. p. xviii
Camborico	m. p. xxxv
Duroliponte	m. p. xxv
Durobrivas	m. p. xxxv

The *Colonia* at the head of the list is Colchester (Camulodunum), *Icinos* the centre of the Iceni at Caister St. Edmund (Venta Icenorum), and *Durobrivas* is Water Newton (Hunts.). Although it is not inconceivable that between Caistor and Water Newton the road followed a more direct line to the north across the Fens—and certainly the east–west Fen Causeway is well attested—the fact that the distance between Cambridge and Water Newton along the Roman road of 36 miles matches closely the 35 miles of the Antonine Itinerary between *Duroliponte* and *Durobrivas* suggests that the former place is Cambridge. The identification of *Camboricum* (for *Camboritum*) with Hockwold-cum-Wilton (Norf.) or perhaps better with Lackford (Suff.) agrees well with the mileage, although the complete road pattern has not so far been established.

The possibility that either *Durcinate* or *Durovigutum*, listed in the Ravenna Cosmography between Colchester and Water Newton, might refer to Cambridge cannot altogether be discounted. There is now no support for the once popular identification of *Camboricum* with Cambridge.[12]

---

[10] Zosimus, vi. 10; Procopius, *De Bello Vandalico*, i. 2. For the events of the last decade of Roman Britain see C. E. Stevens, in *Athenaeum* (Pavia), xxxv (1957), 316–47.

[11] *It. Ant.* 474.4–475.1, ed. O. Cuntz, *Itineraria Romana*, i (Leipzig, 1929), 72–3.

[12] A. L. F. Rivet, in *Britannia*, i. 47; R.C.H.M. *City of Camb.* i, pp. lxv–lxvi.

A consideration of the name *Duroliponte* has suggested that the first element is British and means 'walled town, enclosed town with gateways', while the second contains not the Latin *pons* (bridge) but a British word meaning 'wet, flowing' (cf. Latin *liquidus*, Welsh *gwlyb*), possibly representing a river-name, the whole name being perceived by Roman officials as a locative-ablative of *pons*.[13] Since none of the Antonine Itinerary appears to be later than the 3rd century it is unlikely that the element 'walled town' can refer to the surviving defences of Roman Cambridge, now dated from archaeological evidence to the mid 4th century. As has recently been suggested, it is possible that the place-names incorporating the element *duro-* borne by some towns of Roman Britain were acquired from the comparatively short-lived Roman forts maintained in the neighbourhood during the early Roman period.[14] Moreover the suggestion has, in the case of Cambridge, been strengthened by the identification there of such an early Roman fort.[15]

2. Salinae

A place attributed to the Catuvellauni by Ptolemy (II 3, 11: Σαλῖναι) and located by him near the Wash at a distance of 120 miles from London, the name has been taken as evidence for an early development of salt-working under official supervision in the northern fenlands.[16] On the other hand, the distance of Ptolemy's Salinae from London is close to the actual distance (110 miles) between London and Droitwich (Worcs.), which is the Salinae named in the Ravenna Cosmography. It is perhaps prudent to admit the greater probability that Ptolemy's Salinae is after all also the well-known salt-working centre at Droitwich, sited on the wrong bearing, although at the right distance, from London.[17]

3. River Metaris (? Well Stream)

The Μεταρὶς εἴσχυσις (*Metaris aestuarium*) of Ptolemy (II 3, 4) is evidently the Wash. By implication it identifies a river which flows into the Wash as the Metaris, which may have been the Well Stream or perhaps the whole group of rivers entering the main fen estuary.[18]

Military Remains

Traces of Roman military activity in the county are few. The military fort at Cambridge may belong to the aftermath of the Boudiccan rebellion. The recorded objects of military origin are later than the conquest period and may be associated with the use of Roman troops simply as police. It is significant that they come from the fenlands and, if that area was indeed largely imperial domain, it is to be expected that some forces were placed there to police it and protect supply lines.

A bronze parade helmet from Witcham Gravel, Witcham (approx. TL 458825), is assigned to the late 2nd or early 3rd century. It was lined with iron and had cheek pieces and forehead and neck guards.[19] An iron sword with a fluted bone handle was found beneath deposits containing pottery from the 2nd to the 4th century at Funtham's Lane, Whittlesey (TL 238968).[20] At Church End, Cottenham (TL 470689), an iron

[13] K. Jackson, in *Britannia*, i. 72–3.
[14] *Britannia*, ii (1971), pp. xvi–xvii.
[15] See p. 39.
[16] Hallam, in *Roman Fenland*, 70, 74; below, p. 61.
[17] Rivet, *Town and Country in Roman Britain*, 132, and in *Mélanges offerts à Roger Dion* (*Caesarodunum*, ix bis, ed. R. Chevallier, Paris, 1974), 71.

[18] Salway, in *Roman Fenland*, 19 n. 2. The river Witham which also flows into the Wash cannot be left out of the reckoning: Rivet, in *Mélanges Dion*, 65.
[19] Fox, *Arch. Camb. Region*, 215; cf. *B.M. Roman Britain Guide* (1958), 67 and plate xxvi, 6; *Roman Fenland*, 216.
[20] *J.R.S.* lvi (1966), 209 and plate ix (5).

ballista bolt and what may have been sling stones were associated with pottery of the late 3rd and 4th centuries.[21]

In the late Roman period detachments of troops on stand-by from the bases of the Saxon Shore may have been stationed inland, but their quarters cannot now be recognized.

Dykes

The Cambridgeshire dykes, i.e. the Devil's Ditch, the Fleam Dyke, and the Bran (or Heydon) Ditch, have been claimed as constructions of the late Roman period,[22] either as the work of Romans in the 5th century against English settlers or *foederati*, or of English in the 6th century as defences against renewed British pressure.[23] The latter date is now more widely favoured. Excavation at the Devil's Ditch by the Newmarket racecourse yielded a coin of later than *c.* 350 sealed within the old land-surface below it. A claim that English burials, possibly of the 5th century, might have been dug into the filled-in Fleam Dyke at Bottisham Fen has now been discounted because of the problems of dating and the dubious association of the finds.[24] The two sections of the Fleam Dyke are generally held to be separate constructions.

THE PHYSICAL ENVIRONMENT

The Fenlands, p. 6. South Cambridgeshire, p. 8. Drainage, p. 11.

The Fenlands[1]

THE fenland basin has been eroded out of soft clays of the Oxford, Ampthill, and Kimmeridge formations, all of the Jurassic age; a local development of Corallian limestone forms a small inlier at Upware. The skirt of the fenlands consists of younger Cretaceous rocks, notably the Lower Greensand, Gault, and the Lower Chalk, which form some of the islands. The cover of Pleistocene superficial deposits consists largely of marine March gravels, terraced river gravels, Glacial Sand and Gravel, boulder clay, and early alluvium. Above both the eroded solid formations and the Pleistocene levels are the following Holocene deposits (beginning with the most recent):

i. Alluvial silt and wash, thin deposits of modern river alluvium, recent flood deposits, rainwash, and snow melt.

ii. Peat formed after the Roman period and now largely wasted away.

iii. Alluvium (3) consisting of a silty clay along the Old West River to Setchel Fen, Middle Fen Willingham, and Causeway Farm. It is designated recent alluvial clay on geological maps, and dates from the mid 3rd century A.D. onwards.

iv. Alluvium (2) which forms a roddon[2] marking the old course of the Ouse north-east of Earith and a clay ridge representing a tributary of the old Ouse from Causeway Farm. To the same geological horizon belong also abandoned channels of the Cam in Swaffham Prior Fen and North Fen, Stuntney, near Upware.[3]

[21] *Roman Fenland*, 201: 'These military objects might add some significance to the place-name *Alboro* in the locality.'
[22] Lethbridge, in *Proc. C.A.S.* li (1958), 1–5.
[23] *Arch. Jnl.* cxxiv (1967), 228.
[24] Lethbridge, in *Proc. C.A.S.* li. 1–5.
[1] *V.C.H. Cambs.* i. 1–34. The investigations of the Fenland Research Cttee. have greatly increased knowledge of the Roman environment. This section draws extensively

on them, notably S. C. A. Holmes, 'Outline Geology of the Roman Fenland and Stratigraphy of the Holocene Deposits near the Old West River', *Roman Fenland*, 127–31.
[2] i.e. a meandering bank of laminated silt: cf. *P.N. Cambs.* (E.P.N.S.), 257.
[3] Designated by Holmes, in *Roman Fenland*, 129, as the results of decay in the Roman period or later. Some alluvium may antedate the shell marl with Chara.

v. Shell marl with Chara, whose location indicates the former development of shallow meres.

vi. Peat mainly of post-Bronze Age date occupying deep hollows and channels, which probably had a restricted lateral development in the early Roman period.

vii. Alluvium (1) consisting of clay, silt, peat, peaty loam, and stony sand, which can range in date from Pleistocene to the present day.

In the west part of the South Level a sequence has been established, in which alluvium (1) was formed according to the drainage pattern of the Ouse and Cam, which had been shaped in the Pleistocene period, and accumulated also in the tributary valleys. During the Bronze Age deposition of marine silt in the north led to flooding in the south. In the Iron Age settlement was restricted as water-logging caused peat and shallow meres to form. In the early Roman period the course of the Great Ouse curving north-east of Earith, with a tributary originating from Causeway Farm to join at Willow Farm, is indicated by alluvium (2) flanked on the east by the shell marl of meres and pools. In Willingham mere the strata are, from latest to earliest, the clayey alluvium (3) above shell marl with Chara (5) over peaty silt or clay (6).

Alluvium (3) is a transgression deposit of the mid 3rd century resulting from the breakdown of the Roman drainage. Significantly it spreads eastwards along the course of the present Old West River, that is against the contemporary drainage which has probably been artificially created, and indicates the point at which the breakdown first occurred. Several meres were filled, Willingham and Queen Holme partly so, and the deposit spread north-eastwards a little beyond Snow's Farm and College Farm. More was deposited north-eastwards, against the natural drainage of the Ouse, from the Hermitage into the fen from Willow Farm to Causeway Farm. It pinches out east of Lockspit Hall and the last trace is known c. ½ km. north-west of Twenty Pence Ferry. The deposition of alluvium (3) was not simultaneous, and the main eastward movement to beyond Stretham Mere occurred at an early stage. During most of the post-Roman period the southern fenlands have been waterlogged.[4]

The Neolithic fen clay is overlaid by the Upper Peat, a transition dated to the second half of the 3rd millennium B.C. through the discovery of Early Bronze Age artefacts from the lower levels of the latter. The deposition of estuarine clay on the Upper Peat, which began between 1300 and 300 B.C., prevented the formation of peat seaward of a line between King's Lynn and Denver (Norf.) and along the natural watercourses to Welney and Flaggrass. A rise in the relative sea-to-land level increased the marine element in the deposit, and marine silts and saltmarsh clays were laid over the estuarine clay. The limit of marine deposit occurred during the later Iron Age and the process had ended by the 2nd century A.D. During the Iron Age the siltlands formed a large estuary with wet peatlands inland. Settlement was possible only on the higher ground of the fenland skirt and islands. The line of the coast during this period has been obscured by later deposits.[5] Roman settlement spread to the flats and levées of the Bronze and Iron Age transgression probably in the late 1st century A.D. Between the 2nd and the 4th centuries there is no evidence of marine sedimentation in lands above O.D. In the south fenlands, however, there is substantial evidence for freshwater flooding during the 3rd century, beginning even in the late 2nd. Then ditches became choked with silt and in the siltlands there was a shift to seaward from settlement on the fen edge.

Among the soils of the silt fens, for example in the Wisbech area, lighter silts occur

---

[4] For details of the sequence of deposition see D. M. Churchill, in *Roman Fenland*, 132–42, emphasizing the degree of local variation, especially in the freshwater flooding of the 3rd cent. A.D.

[5] Salway, in *Roman Fenland*, 6 fig. 1(b), 8–9.

towards the mouth of the estuary while the medium and heavy clays, on which were the Roman settlements, lay furthest inland. The silts also attracted settlement on their dry levées. The surrounding soil was fertile and the land required little preparation since it was devoid of trees. Peat areas provided fuel, fodder, thatch, and birds and fish for food, while higher zones afforded summer pasture. It appears that the coastline in Roman times was similar to that of the early Middle Ages. Most of the rivers that now enter the Wash by King's Lynn once flowed into a large estuary north of Wisbech which in the Iron Age had extended further south nearly to Littleport. The limit of settlement in the fenlands, to judge from absence of finds, appears to coincide with *c.* 2 metres O.D., probably the expected limit of seasonal inundation.[6]

South Cambridgeshire

Three zones can be recognized, the claylands, the chalklands of the East Anglian Gateway, and the valleys of gravel and alluvium, each influencing the Roman environment through their soils and vegetation. In the matter of drainage most of the gravels, the chalklands, and the Lower Greensand have soils that are reasonably permeable. Alluvium and chalk marl soils are less so, while the boulder clay, Gault, Kimmeridge, Ampthill, and Oxford clays tend to be impermeable.[7]

There are two major areas of chalky boulder clay, one in the south-east based on chalk and the other in the west on Gault and Jurassic clays. In the south-east soils are mainly clay loams, and although the subsoil is largely impermeable they are lighter and drain better than those in the west. On the south-east the slopes on the chalk are gentler than in the north-west. The south-east claylands have proved more fertile than the western ones and have been cultivated more intensively during the historic past. Finds of Roman material indicate a greater exploitation of small areas than was thought previously. In contrast to the south-east, where land is suitable for both cattle and crops, the western plateau with its heavier clay soils is less productive and the land is wetter and prone to waterlogging in winter. There is more pasture in the west and it is likely that in Roman times the land was used more for cattle than tillage, although sufficient cereals could have been produced for the likely Roman population. In elevation the zone between the clay uplands and the fenland basin is occupied by the chalk downlands. The soft limestone of the Upper Chalk is covered mainly by boulder clay but where that is not so soils range from thin chalk to brown and grey loams, according to the proximity of the boulder clay and its derivatives. In recent times it has been typical sheep and barley land.

The Middle Chalk consists of gentle downland between 30 and 60 metres, cut in places by the Cam valleys and covered here and there by isolated patches of gravel. At the base is the ridge of harder Melbourn rock. There also soils range from thin chalk on the slopes to deeper, sandy brown loams in the more horizontal lower parts, the classical downland favoured for sheep and barley, although the great variation in soils, especially in the amount of calcium carbonate in gravel derived soils, forbids assertions about its general agricultural potential.

The Lower Chalk, which lies between 15 and 30 metres, is divided by several streams. Its base is marked by a band of Totternhoe Stone where a spring-line occurs and the range of soils is narrower than for the Middle Chalk, with more brownish grey soils of a higher chalk content and fewer warm brown soils. Although the greater chalk content makes them more difficult to work their agricultural potential is similar to that

[6] Salway, in *Roman Fenland*, 2–3, 6 fig. 1(a), and General Distribution Map of sheet K.

[7] For this section see H. H. Nicholson and F. Hanley, *Soils of Cambs.* (Min. of Agric. and Fish, Bull. no. 98, H.M.S.O. 1936); R. W. Hey and R. M. S. Perrin, *Geol. and Soils of Cambs.* (1960).

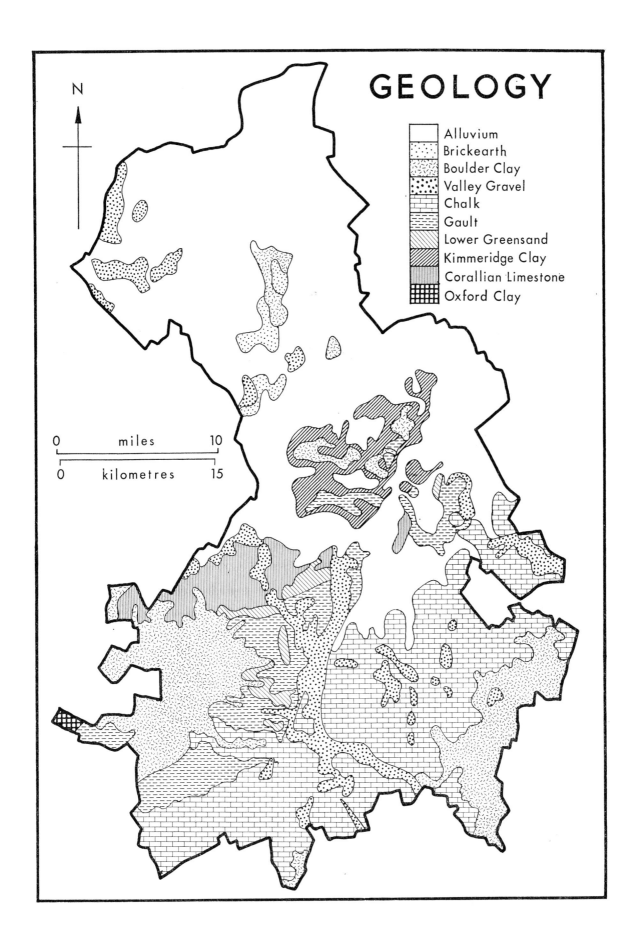

GEOLOGY

- Alluvium
- Brickearth
- Boulder Clay
- Valley Gravel
- Chalk
- Gault
- Lower Greensand
- Kimmeridge Clay
- Corallian Limestone
- Oxford Clay

miles 0 10

kilometres 0 15

of the Middle Chalk with perhaps a higher proportion of grazing. Since the land is less prone to drought, yields tend to be higher. The Chalk Marl between 8 and 20 metres forms a low plain at the foot of the chalk ridges with soils of grey marly loam, the heaviest of the chalk-based soils, although there is some variation in texture and colour, especially when the chalk marl is covered by patches of thin drift. Although drainage can be a problem, good management and use of manure can produce high yields in a wide range of crops. Supply of water often determines the site of settlement on the chalk, which tends to concentrate towards the borders of the claylands and the valleys and along the spring-lines at the junctions between different deposits.[8]

Soils on the Gault include clay and clay loams, ranging from heavy clays to medium loams where there has been contamination with gravel or Lower Greensand. They have a high level of calcium carbonate and organic material but tend to be wet, except during dry weather, and elaborate drainage is required to make the land agriculturally productive. Although capable of high yields of wheat the land tends to remain under grass, permanent or long-term leys.

Restricted areas of soil on Kimmeridge Clay vary from clay loams to medium loams, lighter and more easily worked than soils on Oxford Clay but less fertile than those on Gault because of a deficiency in calcium carbonate. Drainage can also be a problem. Similarly the clays and clay loams on Ampthill and Oxford clays, those in the latter being especially heavy, are less fertile with a lower level of calcium carbonate. Wet in winter and spring because of impeded drainage the land is poor and lies in permanent grass, in which the better varieties are inhibited by water grass.

On the scattered outcrops of greensand, for example in the Gamlingay area, soils are light with a high content of coarse sand and suffer from drought: without improvement they are not fertile and sustain only heathland vegetation. Around Lolworth, Oakington, and Cottenham the soils on greensand are contaminated by neighbouring claylands and tend to be heavier, either loamy sands or loams, and being less acid and more retentive of water are more fertile than other greensand soils. Light or medium loams on the 'island' of Coral Rag and Corallian Oolite between Upware and Barway have a good content of calcium carbonate and drain freely.

The gravels, especially those of the valleys, were the areas of greatest settlement.[9] The soils have been described as 'pale brownish-grey to almost black, gravelly, loamy sands to light loams, over similar but brighter coloured subsoils, lying on a material that is as a rule highly calcareous, but may vary from sandy gravel to marly clay'.[10] In the valley of the Cam above Shelford and those of the Rhee and Bourn, basin-like conditions of drainage prevail, where waterlogging and periodic flooding can occur. When the gravel is thickly deposited drainage is good but where thin deposits overlie impervious strata drainage has to be introduced. Along the fen edges the valley gravels are liable to flooding. Soils of the Old River Gravel have been described as 'from dark brownish-grey to greyish black, loamy sands to medium loams, over brighter coloured subsoils lying on materials which vary from calcareous sands and gravels through calcareous marls to grey clays'.[11] They drain quite freely, except for thin deposits adjacent to clay, and some light soils suffer from drought when the water-table is low. Acidity and limited calcium carbonate can reduce the fertility of gravel soils, although

---

[8] Water is obtained from the Lower Greensand and the Chalk. In recent times the former has been tapped with artesian and sub-artesian wells, and there are wells in the chalk marl. In the Middle Chalk the Cam valley is the major source. Shallow wells were dug in the alluvium and low-lying gravels, and are found at the bases of the chalk formations. In the boulder clay of the south-east wells are fairly shallow and the supply is poor, as in other clay lands.

[9] For the gravels see Geol. Surv. Maps 1″, drift, sheets 187–8, 204–5 (1932–70 edns.); B. C. Worssam and J. H. Taylor, *Geol. of Country around Camb.* (Memoirs of Geol. Surv. 1969).

[10] Nicholson and Hanley, *Soils of Cambs.* 63.

[11] Ibid. 69.

in the main they can produce a wide range of crops and provide pasture for livestock. The land was easy to clear and much had probably been opened up before the Roman conquest.

In the Roman period vegetation of the claylands was oak and ash in varying densities, thinning to scrub at the margins. The natural cover of the Chalk remains conjectural and is likely to have been already extensively modified by man, as was certainly the case with the gravel lands. Most probably grassland was widespread.

Drainage

In Roman times the drainage of Cambridgeshire was substantially different from that of today, especially in the fenlands. The complicated changes of pattern cannot be presented here, not least because they are far from being fully understood, and comment is restricted to the principal elements of the system. The most important single change appears to have been in the course of the Great Ouse: in the early Roman period that river ran by the now extinct West Water branch along the western boundary of north Cambridgeshire, but it was later diverted across the middle of the county into the lower part of the river Cam.

It has been argued that the course of the Cam between Cambridge and Little Thetford is very old, preceded possibly only by an old run on the east side of the Cam between Swaffham and Bottisham lodes and by an abandoned meander on the east at Upware. Below the Newmarket railway bridge at Ely the present course is a relatively recent artificial cut to Littleport. There may be a Roman cut between Littleport and Brandon Creek. North of Southery ferry the course looks to be less artificial, although the meander pattern is less pronounced than might be expected from a natural course.[12] The ancient course from the Newmarket railway bridge passes in a succession of meanders by Stuntney, Thorney Hill, and Quanea Hill to Prickwillow. Until diverted in the 19th century the original channel was flowing between the Old Plough inn and Littleport, and between the latter and Tipps End it is indicated by a depression up to 42 metres wide. Several Roman settlements are known close to that course. In the early Middle Ages the river was navigable up to St. Giles's church, Cambridge, and in the mid 17th century it was tidal up to Ely. As that is likely to have been the case in Roman times the river Cam presumably served as a means of transport for the south part of the county.

South and east of the Cam, between Wicken and Wilbraham, the natural drainage before the construction of the lodes during the Roman period consisted of a major stream, with several minor tributaries originating around the fen edge. The major stream flowed northwards across the fens roughly parallel with the Cam until southeast of Upware where it turned westwards to join the Cam, forming a dendritic pattern of small streams with wet ground intervening. In the Roman period three, or possibly six, artificial lodes were cut across the area. The lodes of definite or probable Roman date are Bottisham, Swaffham Bulbeck, and Reach; those possibly Roman are Wicken, Monk's, and Burwell Old Lode. Except for Wicken and Monk's all the lodes were cut across the natural drainage at a right angle, and had the effect of breaking up the original stream by diverting its flow prematurely into the Cam, the upper part by Bottisham, the middle by Swaffham Bulbeck, and the lower by Reach Lode.[13] Wicken

---

[12] G. Fowler, 'Fenland Waterways', *Proc. C.A.S.* xxxiii (1933), 108–28; xxxiv (1934), 17–33.

[13] R.C.H.M. *Cambs.* ii, pp. liv–lv and figs. 6–7. The lodes may have served for both transport and drainage. Reach Lode has numerous associated Roman finds: Fox, *Arch. Camb. Region*, 180; Fowler in *Proc. C.A.S.* xxxiii.

114. The Devil's Ditch was attached to Reach Lode not later than the early Anglo-Saxon period. The medieval commerce of Reach village (export of clunch, wood, iron, and agricultural produce, import of building stone from Northants.) suggests likely Roman commerce: *V.C.H. Cambs.* ii. 360; R.C.H.M. *Cambs.* ii, pp. lxv–lxvi.

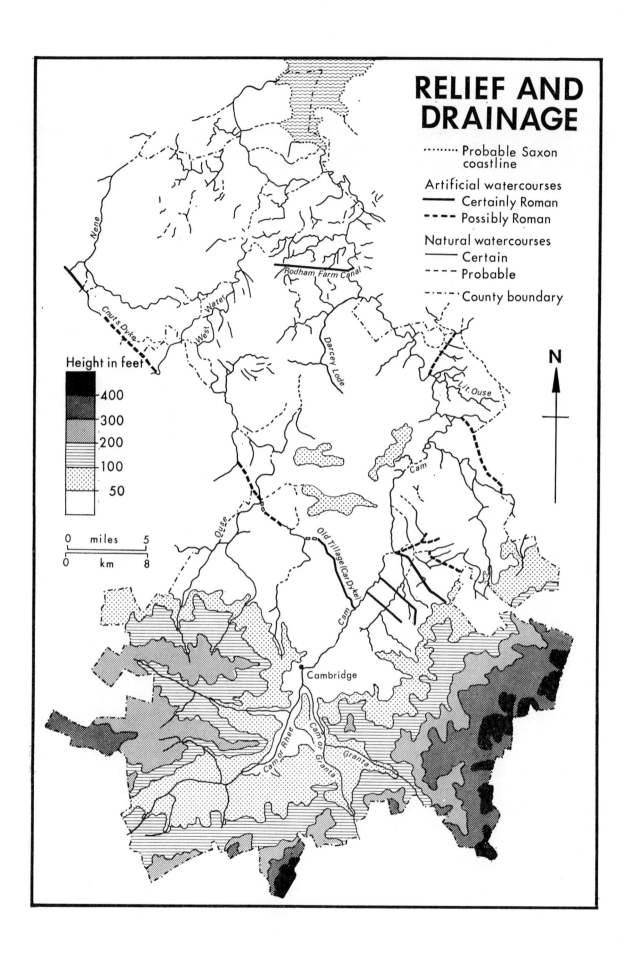

RELIEF AND DRAINAGE

.... Probable Saxon coastline

Artificial watercourses
——— Certainly Roman
- - - - Possibly Roman

Natural watercourses
——— Certain
- - - - Probable
-··-··- County boundary

N

Height in feet

400
300
200
100
50

0   miles   5
0   km   8

Nene

Cnut's Dyke

West Water

Rodham Farm Canal

Darcey Lode

Lit. Ouse

Cam

Ouse

Old Tillage (Car Dyke)

Cam

Cambridge

Cam or Rhee

Cam or Granta

Granta

and Monk's Lode connect uplands around Wicken to Reach, and Burwell Old Lode flows from the fen edge north of Burwell to natural streams leading to Reach Lode.

The river Snail originally flowed northwards to a confluence with the Lark but was diverted to Soham by artificial channels possibly in the 17th century. In antiquity the Lark left its present course at Swale's Fen, north of Isleham, to join the old course of the Cam (TL 575811), a course later superseded by an artificial cut representing the present course of the Lark (to approx. TL 640765) by the 'Old Slade' through Basker-bay which then rejoined the present course (TL 624797) and with a change of alignment flows to a tributary of the Cam at Sindallthorpe House (TL 604830). Finds of Roman pottery from dredging between Lark Hall and Mile End and a find of pewter suggest that the artificial cut may be of Roman date. A complex of artificial and natural watercourses connected to the Lark east of Prickwillow and south of Shippea Hill probably include some channels of Roman date.[14]

The Old Tillage is the more correct name for the waterway generally known as the Cambridgeshire Car Dyke.[15] In its present form it has the appearance of a damp ditch, but originally it was a flat-bottomed dyke containing slowly moving water with gravel banks broken by gaps at fording places. It starts from the Cam (TL 496641) and reaches to Setchel Fen north of Cottenham. A section across the dyke at the Lodge, Water-beach, revealed remains of a Saxon hut on the berm together with residual Roman pottery, while a *terminus post quem* for its construction is furnished by Belgic pottery sealed beneath the north bank at Cottenham. Roman pottery from the basal silt was formerly held to indicate a 1st-century date for construction but more recent studies have suggested a date in the early 2nd century.[16] Although the upper filling contains pottery which could have been deposited any time after A.D. 360 the gravel infill which blocked the dyke as a waterway is probably not earlier than the mid 4th century. It seems very likely that in the early decades of the 4th century coffins in Barnack stone and building stone for the town wall were reaching Cambridge by the Car Dyke.[17] The dyke is thought to have been cut to allow movement between the Cam and the Ouse before the Old West River came into existence to provide a link between Earith (Hunts.) and Little Thetford. Although the stretch of the Old West River between the junction with the Car Dyke (approx. TL 460713) and the Cambridge Road bridge (TL 501722) was formerly thought to be post-Roman,[18] it now seems that it was in the 3rd century A.D. that freshwater floods breached the westward-flowing dyke and created the eastward-flowing Old West River.[19]

Part of the West Water known sometimes as the Colne ditch linked the ancient course of the Ouse with the Cranbrook drain. Roman pottery from it suggests that it may have been used for transport as well as serving as a drain for the Ouse floods.[20] Further north the ancient course of the Ouse (the West Water) is joined near Flood's Ferry and Whittlesey Road Farm, March, by the streams of what was once a major natural waterway which can be traced south of Whittlesey island from King's Delph and is connected to the Nene by the artificial King's Dyke and the natural Oakley–Fulham

[14] Fowler in *Proc. C.A.S.* xxxiii. 117; xxxiv. 26; Salway, in *Roman Fenland*, 236. Roman pottery found in quantity apparently associated with the 'Old Slade' may have been in transit: settlements are not recorded near by. There were clunch pits at Isleham and Jude's Ferry.

[15] Stukeley, without ancient authority, was the first to extend the name from the Lincs. Car Dyke: Hallam, in *Roman Fenland*, 78 n. 26.

[16] *J.R.S.* xxxviii (1948), 88–9; Lethbridge, in *Proc. C.A.S.* xxix (1929), 3–4 (Waterbeach); J. G. D. Clark, in

Antiq. Jnl. xxix (1949), 145–63 (Cottenham); B. R. Hartley, 'Dating of Cambs. Car Dyke', in *Roman Fenland*, 126, stressing that the Car Dyke belongs to a ceramic province notable for its intense conservatism in pottery until well into the 2nd cent.; cf. Hartley, in *Proc. C.A.S.* xlviii (1955), 26–39.

[17] Hartley, in *Roman Fenland*, 126, using pottery published in *Antiq. Jnl.* xxix. 145–63.

[18] Fowler, in *Proc. C.A.S.* xxxiii. 119.

[19] John Bromwich, in *Roman Fenland*, 114–26.

[20] Salway, in *Roman Fenland*, 189.

Dyke. The combined course of the abandoned branch of the Nene and the West Water curve north towards the north-west corner of March Island at Grandford House. Through the Nene there is a link with the south terminus of the Lincolnshire Car Dyke, thus making a direct link by water between the fenlands and northern Britain. Whereas the Old Tillage was large enough to have taken so much water as to reduce the Cam to little more than a stream between Waterbeach and Upware, Bottisham and Swaffham Lodes were adequate to make good the loss, a balance which strengthens the impression that all three channels were broadly contemporary, conceived as parts of a planned scheme of water-transport and drainage.[21]

In the north and north-east of the county Darcey Lode runs from Honey Hill along the west side of Manea island. If it was connected with the waterway which flows roughly east–west south of Doddington it would form a link between the West Water and the main system of the Well Stream. In the east fens there is an important group of artificial cuts, where all the rivers, except for the Lynn Ouse, flow into the Well Stream. Several cuts, however, change the courses from the Wisbech to the Lynn outfall, notably the cut from Littleport to Brandon Creek, the Ten Mile Bank River below Brandon Creek, and the artificial Little Ouse from Decoy Fen to Brandon Creek. The floodwaters of the Cam system were also diverted from the Well Stream. Roman pottery has indicated a date for the works in the 2nd century, perhaps during Hadrian's reign (A.D. 117–38).[22] The roddon marking the old course of the Little Ouse departs from the present course (TL 679859) and is followed approximately by the county boundary. After rejoining the present course (TL 666859) it moves south and east (from TL 663860) to meander until reaching the old course of the Cam at Old Bank Farm, Littleport (TL 583867).[23] The artificial course of the Little Ouse (from TL 663860) to the junction with the Ouse at Brandon Creek is probably Roman.[24] The Littleport Cut, the artificial channel of the Ouse from Littleport bridge (TL 576875) to Brandon Creek, is also probably Roman and may be contemporary with the present course of the Little Ouse.[25]

The Rodham Farm Canal, which can be traced westwards to Lesmond House (TL 437983) and even a little beyond, appears to have been linked closely with the Fen Causeway. In the area of West's Farm the canal and the road, which rests on a separate *agger* 70 metres north of the canal, are associated with extensive field systems comprising rectilinear fields to the south whose main drove crosses the canal to join the road (TL 488977). Evidently the canal, which presumably connected with the Well Stream, was the earlier means of local transport but perhaps as a consequence of 3rd-century floods it had been discarded in favour of the road by the late Roman period.[26] The Flaggrass waterway, which runs at almost a right angle to the causeway, reveals its artificial origin through its regular appearance and several sharp changes of course. In the north it may have connected with the West Water.[27] Finally on the border with Lincolnshire the Old South Eau or Dowsdale Bank has a course that is part natural and part artificial, the latter being probably Roman in origin.[28]

[21] Recent work by B. B. Simmons has called in question the use of the Lincs. Car Dyke for transport: *Britannia*, vii (1976), 325–6.

[22] Salway, in *Roman Fenland*, 11–12, 215.

[23] Fowler, in *Proc. C.A.S.* xxxiv. 28 sqq.; cf. Salway, in *Roman Fenland*, 239. Pottery probably from the silt of the Little Ouse roddon suggests that that course was still open in the 4th cent.

[24] Salway, in *Roman Fenland*, 238.

[25] Fowler, in *Proc. C.A.S.* xxxiv. 20; cf. Salway, in *Roman Fenland*, 240.

[26] For full details see Salway, in *Roman Fenland*, 216–18; for the Fen Causeway, below, p. 22.

[27] Salway, in *Roman Fenland*, 216–17. Where causeway and waterway meet, aerial photographs suggest a paved ford. In and around the Flaggrass settlement the waterway had parallel side-ditches which served as fronts to house compounds: ibid. 221.

[28] Ibid. 272.

ROADS

ASIDE from the waterways already described (p. 11), which although especially suitable for bulk transport are likely to have been restricted to special functions in some parts of the county, movement within Cambridgeshire during the Roman period was facilitated by a system of roads which extended across almost all parts of the country.[1]

Ermine Street (route 2b, Royston–Godmanchester)

There is no doubt about the antiquity of the road, whose original construction probably dates from the early years of the Roman occupation when the Roman army (notably Legio IX Hispana) was advancing towards Lincoln and the river Humber. Not only does it have the classically straight Roman alignment, used later for numerous parish boundaries, but its Roman construction has been proved by excavation. Moreover its name, deriving from Earningas, originates in the early English settlement.[2] Its course is now marked largely by the modern Royston–Godmanchester route, and the earlier turnpike may have adhered to it very closely.[3]

Between Royston and Kneesworth it consists of two straight stretches connected by a short north-westerly deviation, with the northern straight aligned slightly more to the west than the southern. North and south of the Kneesworth crossroads the modern road follows a slight arc to the west, probably a deviation from the Roman course. North of the village the return to the straight course is accompanied by a slight change of alignment to the west.[4] North of the 3rd milestone from Royston a slight northerly deviation is followed by a resumption of the straight alignment slightly more towards the west.

The road appears at a raised level at Wimpole Lodge where it meets the road to Cambridge (route 23). The ford at Arrington bridge produced only Roman finds, which were not necessarily later than the 2nd century, indicating its use at that period.[5]

It seems clear that the Roman surveyors, working from south to north, laid down the road as a succession of straight lengths at whose junctions the alignment was moved slightly more to the west in order to achieve the Ouse crossing at Godmanchester (Hunts.), where the destination was the military post. Between Wragg's Farm and

---

[1] In this survey routes are identified by the numbers, where available, in I. D. Margary, *Roman Roads in Britain* (3rd edn. 1973), the basic work of reference. Of earlier studies the most comprehensive for southern Cambs. is the section in Fox, *Arch. Camb. Region*, 161–73. Some roads in south-east Cambs. are to be found in *Roman Roads of SE. Midlands* (1964) compiled by the 'Viatores'. Roads to which numbers have not been assigned have been given an alphabetical notation.

[2] Fox, *Arch. Camb. Region*, 164–5; cf. Margary, *Roads*,

p. 205; for the name, *P.N. Cambs.* (E.P.N.S.), 22–3.

[3] Babington, *Ancient Cambs.* 52; the modern road slightly distorts the line of Ermine Street: Margary, *Roads*, p. 205.

[4] The inclosure map of 1806 suggests that the westward deviation of the road in Kneesworth village results from encroachment by crofts on the E. and the habitual use of the Bassingbourn turning: Cambs. Record Office, Q/RDc 11.

[5] Lethbridge, in *Proc. C.A.S.* xlv (1952), 61.

milestone eleven the line of the road becomes somewhat sinuous with minor deviations and shorter truly straight stretches. Except for that near Coombe Grove Farm all the deviations move the alignment slightly more towards the west.

The section which runs north from Longstowe is aligned somewhat more to the

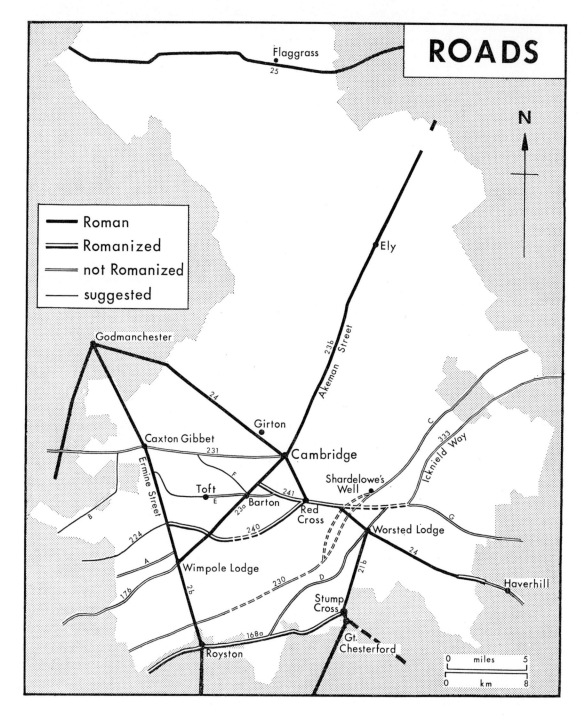

west than the next alignment to the north which begins south of Caxton village. The link was effected by a short length of c. 200 metres aligned east of north, an irregularity that recent roadwork has erased. It is reasonable to conclude that the further course north had already been determined from a survey point near by, and that the line was fixed in three alignments, the northern of which was to the west of the middle alignment beginning about 1 km. south of Caxton Gibbet aiming for a point short of the

8th milestone from Godmanchester. The slight change of alignment at the 9th milestone from Godmanchester at the north end of Caxton village marks the junction of the middle and southern alignments.

From Caxton Gibbet, where Ermine Street crosses the ridgeway (route 231) there is another realignment to the west, aiming the road more directly for Godmanchester. From that point to King's Bush Farm the gradual bend towards the west formed of short straight stretches continues.[6] Between Papworth Everard and north of Lattenbury Hill the county boundary follows the road. A section observed near Lattenbury Hill revealed that the Roman road was 4 metres wide and in places raised to a level of 0·75 to 1 metre.[7]

The final stretch leading into Godmanchester may have been distorted by the building of the modern road. A change of direction at the entrance to King's Bush does not make directly for the town but changes course four or five times before entering by the London road.[8]

The 'Via Devana' (route 24, Godmanchester–Cambridge, Cambridge–Haverhill)

The name *Via Devana* is an antiquarian invention for a road that was once believed to run direct from Colchester to Chester, a hypothesis that now appears to be unfounded.[9] For almost the entire length between Godmanchester and Cambridge the Roman line is followed by the modern road. From Godmanchester it runs straight to near the now destroyed Roman barrow named Emmanuel Knoll, where a section revealed its construction as a core of cobble stones and flint set in mortar.[10] Between there and Gore Tree Farm, opposite Hemingford Abbots (Hunts.), two slightly curving alignments can be observed, which may be original and thus indicate that the road was first surveyed from the direction of Cambridge.[11] After a change of alignment in the south-west end of Fenstanton village (Hunts.) the road heads south-eastwards in direct line to Cambridge which, with gradual changes of line, it enters as the modern Huntingdon Road. For most of its length north-west of Cambridge it is raised about 1·00 metre above ground level.[12] Like Ermine Street it may have been constructed in straight lengths with changes of alignment at their junctions. Such a point may be recognizable about 300 metres south of the crossing of the road from Oakington to Dry Drayton, where a slight diversion to the south brings the road in line to Cambridge; minor changes of direction can be detected elsewhere.

South-east of Cambridge recent work on Wool (or Worsted) Street appears to have produced clear evidence that although the roads north-west and south-east of Cambridge have the superficial appearance of an entity they are really quite independent in origin. The principal reason for building the road south-east from Cambridge may have been access to the Icknield Way (see below) leading into Norfolk towards Hockwold cum Wilton (Camborico) and Caister by Norwich (Venta Icenorum).[13]

---

[6] See Plate I. Changes of alignment occur south of the 7th milestone from Godmanchester, opposite the moat in Papworth Everard, near the 6th milestone, 300 metres south of the Eltisley turning (Papworth Everard), at two places in Lattenbury Hill in Papworth St. Agnes, at the entrance to Lattenbury Farm in Hemingford Abbots, and *c*. 400 metres south of the entrance to Debden Farm in Godmanchester.

[7] T. Codrington, *Roman Roads in Britain* (3rd edn. 1918), 117. It consisted of *c*. 12 cm. of earth covered successively by clay and gravel, *c*. 25 cm. of flints and cobbles set in mortar, and 15–20 cm. of sand and gravel.

[8] Ermine Street appears to have been built after the destruction of the Roman fort at Godmanchester but before the Boudiccan rebellion: H. J. M. Green, in *Small Towns of Roman Britain*, ed. W. Rodwell and T. Rowley (B.A.R. 15, 1975), 185.

[9] The name was bestowed by Chas. Mason (d. 1762), prof. of geography at Camb. For the growth of the theory cf. P. C. Dewhurst, 'Wool Street, Cambs.', *Proc. C.A.S.* lvi–lvii (1964), 56–9. The evidence for the road's Roman origin, which is not in doubt, is summarized in Fox, *Arch. Camb. Region*, 168.

[10] F. G. Walker, in *Proc. C.A.S.* xiv (1910), 163.

[11] Margary, *Roads*, p. 210, suggesting 'errors in setting out'.

[12] Ibid.

[13] A. L. F. Rivet, in *Britannia*, i. 47 n. 40.

The exit from Cambridge was probably on or near Castle and Magdalene streets to a bridge over the Cam.[14] Traces of a wooden causeway, along the east side of Bridge Street, have been suggested as a Roman construction to cross the marsh ground to St. Sepulchre's, whence the line is uncertain but probably followed Sidney, St. Andrew's, and Regent streets and Hills Road, diverging from the last near the Station Road junction to cross the grounds of Homerton College and the Perse School. Excavation in the school playing-fields revealed the road base as *c.* 20 cm. of hard-packed chalk capped with *c.* 70 cm. of earth, gravel, and chalk, with flanking ditches set 14 metres apart.[15] From a T-junction near the new Addenbrooke's Hospital, close to an enclosure of the late Iron Age, the road was once visible as a ridge and beneath a hedge as far as Red Cross, whence the line is mainly that of Worts' Causeway until a change of alignment (TL 489548) brings it on the line of Wool Street north of the Gog Magog golf course.[16]

Much detailed investigation has taken place to determine the origins and character of Wool Street. That it was a Roman road is not in question but while the hypothesis that it incorporated the vallum of a pre-Roman dyke remains unproved the notion that it was a dyke of Saxon times has not been confirmed by excavation.[17] Sections across the road have revealed a variety of detailed information of the materials and methods of construction. Near the north-east angle of the golf course the crest of the ramp was 3·50 to 4 metres wide, without side ditches, and a section revealed the following materials: on the natural chalk 10 cm. of puddled chalk and rammed earth, 35 cm. of earth with a few lumps of chalk, 15 cm. of hard-rammed chalk, capped with 27 cm. of solid gravel, forming a total make-up of *c.* 90 cm. The method of construction was to create a ramp of turf over a platform of rammed chalk. The ramp was rammed down hard, was allowed to settle, and was covered with clean chalk to serve as the bed for the wearing surface of gravel. In the last stage the slopes of the *agger* thus formed were covered with a layer of earth. A hollow traceable on the north side of the road for *c.* 575 metres was examined and found to be a basin-shaped ditch from which the chalk for the road, and for a bank which ran parallel to the road, was extracted. Although no Roman finds were made the method of construction leaves little doubt that the road is Roman.[18] A second section revealed an almost identical construction, again with no Roman finds.[19] An earlier section, made in 1910 at the south-east end of Wool Street, revealed the ramp to be made of rammed chalk, clay, and gravel, on which were laid successively large flints and boulder-clay stones, 35 cm. of packed earth with small flints and stones, and the wearing surface of large flints and stones. The road was about 4 metres wide and flanked by ditches; that on the west measured 1·20 metres wide and 1 metre deep, and contained some Roman objects, including samian pottery and coins.[20]

Extensive trenching for a gas main along almost the entire length of Wool Street has added more detail on the construction of the road, not all of which is consistent with accounts of earlier excavations.[21] At the Worsted Lodge junction it was possible to

[14] For details of discoveries in and around Camb. see D. M. Browne, 'Arch. Gaz. of City of Camb.', *Proc. C.A.S.* lxv (1) (1974).

[15] Walker, in *Proc. C.A.S.* xiv. 141–76. At the same time were found traces of a flourishing Roman settlement. Further excavation at TL 46265583 in the same playing-fields in 1952 failed to locate traces of road metal.

[16] Gravel metalling *c.* 8 m. wide has been recorded on the W. side of the Linton road: R.C.H.M. *City of Camb.* i. 6.

[17] For the name and its corruption to Worsted see *P.N. Cambs.* (E.P.N.S.), 31–3. T. McK. Hughes's vigorous assertion of a pre-Roman origin in *Proc. C.A.S.* x (1904),

458, was neither proved nor disproved by Walker, ibid. xiv. 141–76. Lethbridge's suggestion of a Saxon *agger* with a late road on top, *V.C.H. Cambs.* i. 308, is undermined by Walker, in *Proc. C.A.S.* xiv. 161, and Dewhurst, in *Proc. C.A.S.* lvi–lvii, fig. 2, showing that associated ditches lay on both sides of the *agger*.

[18] Fox, in *Proc. C.A.S.* xxiv. 22–3; located at TL 49725425.

[19] Ibid. 26–7; located at TL 50275385.

[20] Walker, in *Proc. C.A.S.* xiv. 161. Horseheath lies on the edge of the boulder clay.

[21] For details see Dewhurst, in *Proc. C.A.S.* lvi–lvii.

obtain some relative dating for the Icknield Way, Wool Street, and the present road from Great Chesterford to Newmarket. The first coincides with a depression in the foundation layer of chalk of Wool Street, which was lowered to avoid obstructing the ancient route. Beneath the modern Newmarket road the basic chalk layer of Wool Street has been broken by disturbances indicating that the Newmarket road was later.[22] At points south-east of Worsted Lodge some interruption of the *agger* and road surface suggested that construction in the Roman period ceased. South-east of Mark's Grave the modern track curves southward and there is evidence that the Roman line ran straight across the chord of the arc thus formed.[23]

Between Cambridge and Horseheath several changes of alignment, mainly to the east of south aiming the road towards Horseheath, provide another example of the Roman practice of surveying in short straight stretches as already noted for the Ermine Street and the Cambridge–Godmanchester road. For most of the distance between Cambridge and Godmanchester the road forms parish boundaries. It is likely that a prehistoric route via Haverhill (Suff.) linked the Colne and Stour valleys with the routes crossing Cambridgeshire from south-west to north-east, but there is no evidence that any such route was adapted to the form of a Roman road.[24] Certainly while the the road between Cambridge and Horseheath was constructed in the Roman fashion nothing similar is known within the county beyond Horseheath. Even south-east of Worsted Lodge the Roman construction remained unfinished for some reason which is not clear.

Akeman Street (route 23b, north of Cambridge)

Although the name is an antiquarian invention the Roman origin of the road is well attested.[25] Presumably departing by a gate in the north-east defences, its line through the built-up area of modern Cambridge is unclear but probably ran west of Stretton Avenue, beyond which it was once visible south-west of Arbury Road[26] as a ridge. North of Arbury Road the ridge was at one point 43 metres wide and 0·80 metre high (TL 45226119) but with a mean width of 20 metres. A section showed that the *agger* was made from brown earth, beneath whose crest an articulated horse skeleton lay on the surface in a hollow in the natural ground. Coincident with the top of the pit was a gravel level identified as later metalling.[27] At King's Hedges on the north boundary of Cambridge the course towards Landbeach is marked by a lane known as the Mere Way, most of which forms a parish boundary. After the lane turns off to Landbeach (at TL 472652) the Roman line is continued as a low *agger* until it is joined by the modern Cambridge–Ely road at Goose Hall, where it crosses the Car Dyke and appears to

---

[22] Ibid. 46–7, figs. 3–4. At Worsted Lodge part of the ditch flanking the road on the SW. is preserved. The present lane there is off the Roman line and above the NE. ditch, creating a misleading impression that the *agger* of the road was a rampart.

[23] Observed as a cropmark in an aerial photograph by Rainbird Clark, 1936. For coal used in constructing Wool Street see below, p. 69.

[24] Cf. Fox, *Arch. Camb. Region*, 168–9; followed by Dewhurst, in *Proc. C.A.S.* lvi–lvii, 44, in the suggestion that several prehistoric routes converged at TL 49255458. A course described by Margary, *Roads*, p. 211, beyond Hare Wood, in West Wickham, to Haverhill, and claimed by Codrington, *Roman Roads*, 193, as traceable 8 km. SE. of Haverhill has the sinuous character of a pre-Roman road rather than that of the uncompleted Roman road SE. of Worsted Lodge.

[25] *P.N. Cambs.* (E.P.N.S.), 18–19.

[26] Botwell records a stone structure outside and just S. of the centre of the E. ramparts of the later castle, which may have belonged to the Roman gate or town wall: Browne, in *Proc. C.A.S.* lxv (1), map 2, no. 6. The ridge is not aligned with a section N. of Arbury Rd. and revealed no trace of metalling or side-ditches when examined in 1953. A slight change of alignment occurred at the Seventh Public Drain: R.C.H.M. *City of Camb.* i. 4.

[27] For the section in Arbury Site IX see Alexander, Excavation Rep. 1968, 1969. A kink in the supposed *agger* (TL 453615) is later than the filling of a 4th-cent. rectangular enclosure, and the axis of the metalled road ran E. of the supposed line. The lack of precise alignment with the section S. of Arbury Rd. probably represents a shift of the crest of the road through agricultural activity. See also below, Plate VIA.

interrupt the channel, which may have been obsolete when the Roman road was built.[28]

From Goose Hall the Roman is followed by the modern road to Chittering chapel, where the latter deviates for about 800 metres from the straight Roman line, which was found to be built of gravel 5 metres wide and flanked by ditches.[29] The crossing of the Ouse (Old West River) has not yet been satisfactorily identified.[30] North of the Ouse the line remains uncertain and there seems grounds for accepting a suggestion that the Roman road was destroyed by later inundation, although the *agger* has been observed in the fields south of Stretham village, within which the line is followed by Short Lane to pass west of the church and rejoin the modern road at the north end of the village (approx. TL 51207495).[31] North of Stretham (TL 51407545) the modern road diverges north-eastwards to Thetford Corner, while the Roman road continues straight across the east end of Grunty Fen.[32] It is generally accepted that 1 km. of the modern road from milestone 66 towards Ely follows the ancient line, and the presence of the road has been shown in Ely itself. The Roman road thus defined takes maximum advantage of higher ground above the fen, which it crosses at the narrowest suitable place. It was clearly possible to reconcile the preference for directness with the minimum of engineering work.[33]

North of Ely some parts of the modern road to Littleport (to TL 536802, TL 540804 to 551835) follow the Roman line but it is not certain that it is represented thereafter by the modern road across Wood Fen. A strip of gravel metalling running north-east from Blue Boar House (TL 562840) towards Pyper's Hill may be the main Roman road or perhaps a branch towards Hockwold. In Littleport the modern road to the Old Croft river (TL 563860 to 568870) is believed to represent the ancient line, where it is also thought to have followed the levée of the Old Croft for about 7 km. On the other hand, if the Littleport alignment is projected northwards it meets the next tributary of the Old Croft river where the road has next been recorded, at Cold Harbour Farm, in Southery (Norf.) (TL 587928).[34]

Cambridge to Ermine Street (Wimpole Lodge) (route 23a)

The road from the 4th-century south-west gate of Cambridge may be a spur connecting with an earlier line making for the bridgehead. It passes east of the old university rifle range and crosses the Madingley road, St. John's playing-fields, Grange Road, and Adams Road, south-west of which it is clearly visible on aerial photographs.[35] Between the area of Barton Farm and Hey Hill south-west of Barton village, where the line is taken up by the modern road to Wimpole Lodge, the Roman road has to be sought

[28] See Margary, *Roads*, p. 209; cf. Walker, in *Proc. C.A.S.* xiv. 154. Three slightly different alignments can be seen SW. of the turn to Landbeach. Between the Cottenham road and Goose Hall the road forms a low ridge across the fields.

[29] Walker, in *Proc. C.A.S.* xiv. 154–5. The clearing of Chittering Beach Ditch, TL 49757042 to 49777047, revealed cambered gravel of the road: *J.R.S.* xlvi (1956), 138. The road serves as a parish boundary NE. of Goose Hall.

[30] Babington, *Ancient Cambs.* 16, proposed a crossing east of the present road, rejected by Fox, *Arch. Camb. Region*, 165; Walker, in *Proc. C.A.S.* xiv. 154, suggested that after the deviation at TL 496699 the modern road regained the Roman line.

[31] It had disappeared by the time of William I's attack on Ely: Walker, in *Proc. C.A.S.* xiv. 154; and the deviation of the modern road at Elford Closes (TL 502726) does not represent a Roman alignment. Margary, *Roads*, p. 209 records the *agger* in fields 1·5 km. S. of Stretham, E. of the road on Middle Common. Codrington, *Roman Roads*, records the Roman road's discovery at Stretham at a depth of 2·25 metres.

[32] Walker, in *Proc. C.A.S.* xiv. 155–6; cf. Margary, *Roads*, p. 209. Traced to Bedwell Hay Farm, where it is represented for *c.* 800 metres by a lane locally called the Roman road. A slight *agger* 8 metres wide is visible near the farm, and rises in hedge-lines and a defined ridge have been observed each side of Grunty Fen.

[33] Babington, *Ancient Cambs.* 19–20; Fox, *Arch. Camb. Region*, 165–6.

[34] Salway, in *Roman Fenland*, 229–30.

[35] For the older names see *P.N. Cambs.* (E.P.N.S.), 18–19; for the line, Browne, in *Proc. C.A.S.* lxv (1). The line is traceable to TL 429578, where a ridge 20 m. wide and 30 cm. high represents the *agger*: R.C.H.M. *City of Camb.* i. 4.

in fields, hedge-lines, and lanes. From Dumpling Farm a ridge is visible in raking light up to the Grantchester–Coton road, which it crosses about 60 metres north of its crossing of the main road. From there the line is visible as a ridge and as rising hedge-lines to a field called Bull's Close near Barton village where excavation revealed the *agger* to consist of a foundation of beaten chalk and gravel covered by boulder stones and cobbles, and by 50 cm. of a mixture of rammed earth, sand, and chalk. A local record of the 19th century describes the road as 4 metres wide and flanked by ditches 1·50 metres wide and 1·00 metre deep, in which Roman pottery and glass were found.[36] From Bull's Close the road is represented by a lane heading for Barton church, which it passes on the west, and continues as a grass track known locally as the 'Roman road'.[37] Passing Hey Hill, where the road has been observed as a ridge, it follows a line near to Lord's Bridge and joins the modern Wimpole Lodge road. Except for a slight deviation at one point (TL 341493) the Roman road is represented by the modern one for the 15 km. to the junction with Ermine Street. South of Hey Hill the road is normally raised at a level of about 75 cm. Three major changes of alignment, incorporating minor readjustments, can be seen between Cambridge and Ermine Street.[38]

Red Cross via Grantchester to the Cambridge–Wimpole road (route 241)

At its east end the road branches from the Cambridge–Horseheath road on the site of the new Addenbrooke's Hospital and is seen as a ridge about 30 metres wide and 30 cm. high in a field between Downing College's fields and those of the Sixth Form College.[39] The line across Shelford Fen to the west is not certain, although visible traces have been claimed east of the Trumpington road, which it crosses, as a bank north of Trumpington village, and as a lane leading to Trumpington Fen where it is once again lost.[40] Some doubt has been cast on the traditional identification of the crossing of the river Cam where a hollow way near Grantchester school points towards the river, because a supposedly Roman earthwork adjacent to it has been proved to be Anglo-Saxon or medieval in origin, although that does not rule out the existence of a pre-Roman or Roman track.[41] The line of the hollow way is continued through Grantchester village by the Coton road until the point where that road turns westward, whence the line is followed by an old bridle-path called Deadman's Way which reaches the Cambridge–Wimpole route (23a) close to the 3rd milestone from Cambridge. An alternative or more likely secondary line has been observed as a bank which runs from south-east to north-west north of Grantchester 700 metres long and 20–3 metres wide and 50–70 cm. high but was found to contain no metalling. It crosses the Grantchester–Coton road and joins the Cambridge–Wimpole road (23a) near cottages on the Barton road west of the Coton turning.[42]

Red Cross via Hauxton to Mare Way (route 240)

The existence of the road, for which the evidence is both meagre and unsatisfactory, has been inferred from the virtually straight alignment of the north boundary of Great Shelford parish near Hauxton mill to its junction with the Hobson brook, whence a

[36] Babington, *Ancient Cambs.* 21, believed that the Roman road joined the modern road near TL 432577; Walker, in *Proc. C.A.S.* xiv. 158–9, where details of construction are given, that the 800 metres of the line SW. of Barton Farm had disappeared.

[37] Babington, *Ancient Cambs.* 21; Walker, in *Proc. C.A.S.* xiv. 160–1, recording a local tradition of a surface of boulder stones beneath the grass track at Barton.

[38] Margary, *Roads*, p. 208. The line turns slightly S. at TL 387538 and slightly W. at Fox Hill (TL 369514).

South of Bourn brook sporadically, and nowhere north of it, the road marks parish boundaries.

[39] R.C.H.M. *City of Camb.* i. 6.

[40] Babington, *Ancient Cambs.* 43; Walker, in *Proc. C.A.S.* xiv. 168.   [41] Alexander, Excavation Rep. 1967.

[42] R.C.H.M. *Cambs.* i, pp. lix–lx; Margary, *Roads*, p. 213. Babington, *Ancient Cambs.* 49–50, cites B.L. Add. MS. 6768 for a paved way, in a field S. of Deadman's Way, of pebbles 30 cm. thick set in gravel with brickwork to the sides, which could be the remains of a Roman road.

projection aims north-eastward towards the Red Cross junction.[43] From the crossing of the east branch of the Cam at Hauxton mill the line is marked by a lane (from TL 424524) to the west branch of the Cam which was probably crossed between Burnt Mill Bridges and River Farm, where part of the original gravel bed of the ford has been recognized.[44] West of River Farm one suggestion has the line running near Money Hill and Mount Balk barrows to the south-east corner of Harlton parish west of Chapel Hill (TL 395518), but a more direct line has been also suggested.[45] From the south-east corner of Harlton parish the line to Fox Hill, where it is crossed by the Cambridge–Wimpole road (23a), is marked by a parish boundary. From Thorn Hill a line curving towards Ermine Street is marked by the Mare Way, where traces of an *agger* 10 metres wide and 30–60 cm. high suggest that it was built up in the Roman manner from an existing pre-Roman ridgeway.[46]

The Fen Causeway (route 25, Peterborough–Denver)

Traces of a Roman road across the north fens branching from Ermine Street to follow a course from Peterborough through Whittlesey, March, and Nordelph (Norf.) to Denver (Norf.) have long been recognized. It enters the county north of Whittlesey and leaves south of Upwell.[47]

From the Cat's Water (the old Nene, at TL 222990, with a change of alignment at TL 220992), where gravel metalling has been found on the south bank, it crosses Fulham's Dyke and after a change of direction joins the Northey road (Thorney) where that turns sharply northwards. Gravel metalling has been observed in a field south of Mason's Farm (TL 233987), parallel to the present road.[48] Following the modern track across the Nene Washes, the line turns eastward (approx. TL 237980) and follows Low Road for *c.* 3 km., after which it is continued by curving field boundaries to the east edge of Whittlesey island. At Eastrea there is a raised gravel causeway where there is a change of direction to Coates island, to the east end of which the line is followed either by the modern road or by Cow Way. Towards Eldernell it is indicated by a footpath and later a lane. Several changes of direction are apparent in banks and ditches preserved in pasture, and there is a line of gravel on low ground towards Long Drove. After a change of alignment (TL 338992) the road disappears but later reappears (TL 351993). In the peaty ground the road was laid on a foundation of brushwood, sealing at one point a coin of Vespasian (A.D. 69–79) to furnish a *terminus post quem.*[49] Traces of gravel at Infield's Farm, in March, and farm tracks mark the line of the road from there to Watt's Farm (TL 376996), whence a line of gravel continues to Grandford Drove (TL 386997). The road is lost until it crosses the West Water north-west of Grandford,[50] and continues as an *agger* south of Grandford House, March, until it turns east (TL 395992) to run beneath the Wisbech–March road. It can be seen on an aerial photograph (TL 398989) heading for the enclosure at Westry Farm west, March (TL 401988), which appears to antedate the road. From east of Westry Farm (TL

[43] Walker, in *Proc. C.A.S.* xiv. 176; Margary, *Roads*, p. 212, observes that the boundary towards Hauxton mill follows the crest of a low ridge.
[44] Fox, *Arch. Camb. Region*, 151, prefers the crossing near River Farm, where he saw traces of a ford, to that at Burnt Mill Bridges suggested by Walker, in *Proc. C.A.S.* xiv. 172.
[45] Walker, in *Proc. C.A.S.* xiv. 172; Fox, *Arch. Camb. Region*, 150, while preferring the more direct line considers the possibility of a track N. of Mount Balk and S. of Money Hill to a ford at Harston mill, and he notes a continuous hedge-line past Money Hill heading for the 'fordway' marked on O.S. Map 1″, sheet 51 (1836 edn.).

[46] For the name Mare Way see *P.N. Cambs.* (E.P.N.S.), 27; for details of the *agger*, Margary, *Roads*, p. 213. There has probably been some distortion of the boundaries in relation to the track between Fox and Thorn hills. Mrs. Pullinger suggests partial Romanization on the evidence of metalling and surface finds of samian and grey ware.
[47] See Margary, *Roads*, pp. 230–2; Salway and others, in *Roman Fenland*, 185–6, 196, 216–18.
[48] W. C. Little, in *Jnl. Brit. Arch. Assoc.* [1st ser.], xxxv (1879), 267–8.
[49] E. M. Beloe, in *Proc. C.A.S.* vii (1893), 118; J. R. Garrood, in *Antiq. Jnl.* xviii (1938), 76–7; *J.R.S.* xxviii (1938), 183. [50] *Roman Fenland*, plate vb.

403988) it runs south-east and a change of alignment brings it east of Elm Road (TL 421984), where excavation revealed a single deposit of metalling above silt. After another change of alignment (TL 426983) it heads to the south of the Flaggrass settlement. After a turn to the north-east it crosses the Old Croft river (the Well Stream) into Norfolk (TL 504983).[51]

Between Peterborough and Denver the width of the road varies in general from 5 to 14 metres and any regularity disappears when it passes through settlements. At Flaggrass (TL 434985) the road broadens to an open area, the ditches are irregular, and there is no trace of metalling. At Grandford, however, the settlement encroaches on the line of the road (TL 393996).

The Icknield Way north-east of Worsted Lodge (route 333)

The Icknield Way was one of the principal prehistoric routes of Britain and it is not surprising that excavation at Worsted Lodge showed it to be earlier than Wool Street. On the other hand, one cannot assume that it was anywhere a single road; it was rather a band of paths and droves, used at different seasons of the year, which followed the open chalk upland from south-west to north-east across the south of the county, remaining below the higher wooded claylands to the south-east.[52] There is no doubt that the Icknield Way continued to be used in Roman times but what is not certain is whether the modern Royston–Newmarket road north of Worsted Lodge represents a Roman regularization of the earlier tracks.[53]

On the evidence of a charter of 974 Fox suggested that the Icknield Way did not cross the Fleam Dyke at the same point as the present road but where the parish boundary of West Wratting and Great Wilbraham touches the dyke near Mutlow Hill, although a trial excavation revealed no causeway across the ditch. It was further suggested that two hollow ways south-west of the dyke, aligned roughly on the Bronze Age barrow on Mutlow Hill, and a continuation of the line by another hollow way north-east of the dyke and barrow represented remnants of tracks which once formed the Icknield Way.[54] While the more precise reconstructions based on the charter of 974 have been questioned it seems reasonable to accept the hollow ways leading towards Mutlow Hill as part of an original Icknield Way, while the crossing of the Fleam Dyke by the present road is certainly secondary and does not therefore represent the line of a Roman road. A few tracks of the Icknield Way, such as the hollow way noted north-east of Mutlow Hill, led in a more northerly direction but most traffic probably followed the line represented by the boundary of West Wratting and Great Wilbraham. Certainly the notion of a regular Roman version of the Icknield Way in the region has no evidence to support it.[55]

---

[51] See Plate IIB. For the historical relationship between the Fen Causeway and the Rodham Farm Canal see Salway, in *Roman Fenland*, 217.

[52] Fox, *Arch. Camb. Region*, 143; for the relation to Wool Street see Dewhurst, in *Proc. C.A.S.* lvi–lvii. 56–9.

[53] Fox, *Arch. Camb. Region*, 166, arguing that no trace of Romanization is apparent at the Fleam Dyke, is sceptical of the road's Roman origin, asserted by Codrington, *Roman Roads*, 191, and supported by Margary, *Roads*, p. 262. R.C.H.M. *Cambs.* ii, p. xxvi, doubts that there was a single road in Roman times. The modern road appears to be a creation of the early 19th cent.

[54] Birch, *Cart. Sax.* iii, pp. 628–9; C. Fox and W. M. Palmer, 'Excavations in Cambs. Dykes', *Proc. C.A.S.* xxiv (1923), 33; xxv (1924), 28–9, interpret the charter as recording two distinct routes, the Icknield Way and the

road followed by the parish boundary between West Wratting and Great Wilbraham, which aligns with the Worts' Causeway section of the road from Cambridge to Worsted Lodge (route 24). Neither of Fox's excavations yielded acceptable evidence of a Roman road.

[55] *P.N. Cambs.* (E.P.N.S.), 26, identifies the 'straet' with the Icknield Way; Lethbridge, in *Proc. C.A.S.* li. 2, identifies it with Ashwell Street passing the dyke at Shardelowe's Well (see below). Fox was unable to discount the evidence for ditches beside the continuation of the parish boundary between the modern road and Fleam Dyke: *Proc. C.A.S.* xxiv. 33. His northern hollow way may have been one of a group of tracks, now largely obliterated, connecting the upland Icknield Way with the lowland Street Way and Ashwell Street routes.

The Icknield Way from Baldock (Herts.) to Stump Cross (route 168a)

It has been shown that from Odsey, in Guilden Morden, to Royston the modern road represents the line of a Romanized Icknield Way until about 400 metres east of the crossing of the London–Cambridge road, where the present road diverges slightly from the ancient line which continues successively as an *agger* and as a hollow way. West of Noon's Folly Farm, Melbourn, the Royston–Newmarket road turns away to the north-east and the Icknield Way continues as a farm lane. From King's Building, where it crosses the Barley–Fowlmere road, it is followed by a sunken lane for about 600 metres then by a field track which diverges (at TL 414419) southwards from the ancient line. East of the Bran (or Heydon) Ditch an *agger* is visible north of the present lane, and where that turns (TL 432422) more towards the south original road-metalling is visible in the fields on the north. The lane later resumes the ancient course (TL 434423) and continues as a minor road followed by the county boundary south of Chrishall Grange, Fowlmere. After an east of south turn at the south-west corner of Chrishall Grange Plantation both the Way and the present road make another turn to the east bringing them to Ickleton as far as the junction with the Duxford road on the west side of the village. East of the village the line may be indicated by a hedge and it crossed the Cam by a ford (TL 449440) from which it is marked by a lane to Stump Cross, where it joins the road from Great Chesterford (Essex) to Worsted Lodge (21b).[56]

Great Chesterford to Worsted Lodge (route 21b)

It has been generally accepted that the present road represents a Romanized stretch of the Icknield Way. Its pre-Flavian date and therefore likely military origin seems to be indicated by its relation to an early military base at Great Chesterford. The road, which is raised at a level of *c.* 60 cm. to 1 metre, follows two straight alignments with a slight change east of north at their junction (TL 521497).[57]

Ashwell Street (route 230)

This road in Roman times linked the Baldock–Godmanchester road with Ermine Street and continued eastwards at least as far as Whittlesford. Though the straight stretches of road which now bear the name may be discounted as creations of the 19th century, it seems reasonable to accept the view that the road was essentially a pre-historic route which continued in use during the Roman period, as indicated by settlements and burials along its course.[58]

From Ashwell (Herts.) to Ermine Street (route 2b) the line is clear, after which a lane has been taken to mark its sinuous course to the point (TL 371438) where the lane turns sharply south of east to join the Melbourn–Royston road.[59] Between Melbourn and Fowlmere the road is generally agreed to follow a southern line beside the marsh once called Melbourn Common and, after touching the north end of the Bran Ditch, follows a farm track to Fowlmere,[60] whence its course is marked by the modern road to Thriplow.[61] East of Whittlesford the line is uncertain and none of the various

[56] For details see *Roman Roads of SE. Midlands*, 66–8 and maps.

[57] The road marks county and parish boundaries for almost its entire length. For the traces of the road at Great Chesterford see Rodwell, in *Britannia*, iii. 290–3 and fig. 1 and plate xxiiia.

[58] See O. G. S. Crawford, *Strip Map of Litlington* (O.S. Professional Papers, 17); *Roman Roads of SE. Midlands*, 238–44; Margary, *Roads*, pp. 207–8.

[59] Fox, *Arch. Camb. Region*, 148; Margary, *Roads*, p. 207, observes than an *agger* visible crossing the fields,

along with the parish boundary, continues the previous line.

[60] Babington, *Ancient Cambs.* 57–8; cf. Margary, *Roads*, p. 207. Fox, *Arch. Camb. Region*, 148, suggests a route N. of the marsh along a track marked on O.S. Map 1″, sheet 51 (1836 edn.), and known in one part as Ashwell Street and in another as King's Lane, perhaps used after the post-Roman construction of the Bran Ditch.

[61] Fox, *Arch. Camb. Region*, map D, indicates a line further S., followed roughly by the Thriplow–Whittles-ford lane which he calls 'Ashwell Street or Street Way'.

suggested routes seems to have much evidence in its favour. One has a line south of Whittlesford which crosses the Cam and continuing by Pampisford and the north end of the Brent Ditch joins the Icknield Way at Bourn Bridge, while another proposes a course to Whittlesford bridge to join a northern line of the Icknield Way via Pampisford and Babraham to Worsted Lodge.[62] Two other suggestions include the line of a path from Whittlesford mill to Sawston, which passes the church and continues as a field path to Copley Hill Farm (previously Cott Farm) in Babraham on the Cambridge–Haverhill road, whence it followed a post-inclosure track to Lodge Farm (Fulbourn) and beyond to Shardelowe's Well (TL 558537) at the end of Fleam Dyke. Alternatively from Sawston church it may have followed a line to the Wormwood Hill barrow by a track to North Farm and a parish boundary, whence it reached the Worsted Lodge road by a sinuous track skirting the Gog Magog park on the south-east and then proceeded straight to Shardelowe's Well.[63] If the road did cross the Cam, then it is difficult to choose between the suggested routes, although if the road was aiming for Shardelowe's Well both lines between Whittlesford mill and the road from Cambridge to Worsted Lodge (Wool Street) have directness in their favour, and indicate the existence of a lower through-route that is more clearly defined than has usually been accepted. On the other hand, it should be borne in mind that all the suggestions rest on the assumption, largely unsupported, of a continuity between Ashwell Street and the Street Way (see below).

The Mare Way west of Ermine Street (route 224)

There is no evidence that this line, of which only the stretch east of Cockayne Hatley (Beds.) is here relevant, formed part of a Roman road, a notion based on its being a continuation westwards of that from Red Cross to Ermine Street via Hauxton (route 240, above).

After a change of alignment 35° to the north, just west of the county boundary, the road ran north-west of a moat (TL 275497) to coincide with a parish boundary, the edge of a wood, and a drive south-west of Home Farm, Hatley St. George. After following the boundary for *c.* 500 metres the line is held to continue across fields until it meets Old Croydon Lane (TL 297519) north-east of Long Lane Farm. The road follows the lane until it turns 30° east to follow a bridle path marked by a parish boundary to a junction with Ermine Street (TL 320529).[64]

Little Brickhill (Bucks.) to Arrington Bridge (route 176)

Of this road, which is held to link the Cambridge–Wimpole road (23a) with the road from Buckingham (166), only the stretch from the Baldock–Biggleswade road (TL 215407) is relevant. A line is proposed along a ridgeway and then along the Dunton (Beds.) road, whence it is held to be followed (TL 22654225) by a green lane, marking parish and county boundaries, to the river Rhee. Across the river the line continues as a drove until changing direction north-east (TL 261415) and following Church Lane which enters Guilden Morden from the south-west. From there it continues as Flecks Lane, then along the present road to Wendy. After passing through the village it is held to rejoin the present road almost to Ermine Street which is joined

[62] Proposed respectively by Babington, *Ancient Cambs.* 58, from Little Shelford to Whittlesford bridge and thence to Bourn Bridge, and by Fox, *Arch. Camb. Region.* 148 and map D.

[63] Both noted by Fox, *Arch. Camb. Region,* 148–9, not accepting that the Cam is likely to have been crossed at Whittlesford mill.

[64] Described in *Roman Roads of SE. Midlands,* 270 and map, p. 486.

a little south of Arrington bridge. Nevertheless the evidence of a Roman road to Arrington bridge from the west is doubtful.[65]

Cambridge via Caxton Gibbet to Croxton (route 231)

There are grounds for accepting the existence of a Roman road west from Cambridge, although its precise course remains uncertain in many places. Superficially the present road from Cambridge to St. Neots exhibits the appearance of a Roman road, at least as far as its crossing of Ermine Street at Caxton Gibbet. The present road runs on a large *agger* from TL 422593 to 415594 and is believed to follow the Roman line as far as Childerley Gate.[66] No trace of the Roman road was found in a trench across the present road near the turning to Bourn (TL 336599), although Roman coffins were found during the building of Bourn airfield south of the road.[67] A hedgerow marking a parish boundary and an old lane are held to mark the Roman line east and west of Caxton Gibbet. On grounds of unspecified surface remains the line is traced to a road-junction north-east of Eltisley, and a hedgerow on an *agger* carries it through the village to the junction of a track from Yelling with the present St. Neots road (TL 269597), which follows it, apart from deviations north and south, to the county boundary and a possible continuation to Bolnhurst (Beds.).[68]

Ermine Street via Tadlow to Biggleswade (route A)

A Roman road (route 222) is known between Biggleswade and Old Warden (Beds.), and an eastward continuation of it has been suggested on the line of the Cambridge–Sandy road from Ermine Street through Tadlow. Although hedge-lines and parish boundaries can, as with routes 176 and 224, amount to a practically continuous line, definite grounds for believing in the existence of a Roman road are still lacking.[69]

Eltisley to Sandy (route B)

A suggested prehistoric ridgeway from Madingley Hill to Eltisley on the line of the St. Neots road may have continued via Great Gransden (Beds.) to Sandy (Beds.), but there is no evidence that the route, though possibly used in Roman times, ever took the form of a Roman road.[70]

The 'Street Way' north-east of Wool Street (route C)

There is no definite evidence for this route, which has been conjectured as part of a through road from Bishop's Stortford (Herts.) to Brancaster (Norf.), since in the county it became a fenced road only during the early 19th century. A suggested track from Worsted Lodge to Shardelowe's Well at the Fulbourn end of the Fleam Dyke, thence to Badlingham, in Chippenham, and Mildenhall (Suff.), has been seen as part of a continuous route linked to the Peddars Way in Norfolk.[71] Between the Fleam Dyke

[65] Described in *Roman Roads of SE. Midlands*, 289. A hollow way can be seen near Manor Farm, Shingay; ibid. 449 map J; a crest has been observed in the same area.

[66] Described ibid. 264–7 and maps, pp. 491–3. The location of the SW. gate of Camb., which it left with the Cambridge–Wimpole road (route 23a) has to be revised: see below, p. 42. W. Liller, in *Proc. C.A.S.* lix (1966), 136, suggests that the road, of which he saw no trace in trenching between Observatory Buildings and Madingley Road as indicated in *Roman Roads of SE. Midlands*, followed Madingley Road to join route 23a W. of Lady Margaret Road.

[67] C. F. Tebbutt, in *Proc. C.A.S.* lviii (1965), 145.

[68] The present road marks the parish boundary for several stretches E. and one short stretch W. of Caxton Gibbet.

[69] Babington, *Ancient Cambs.* 24–5; cf. Margary, *Roads*, p. 204. Fox, *Arch. Camb. Region*, 165, rejects the use by Walker, in *Proc. C.A.S.* xiv. 161, of Baker, *Map of Cambs.* (1821) as evidence for a similar road S. of Tadlow.

[70] Fox, *Arch. Camb. Region*, 154 map v.

[71] Babington, *Ancient Cambs.* 65, proposed a continuous route to the Peddars Way; cf. Fox, *Arch. Camb. Region*, 149–50 and map IV. For 19th-cent. developments see R.C.H.M. *Cambs.* ii, p. xxvi.

and the Running Gap in the Devil's Ditch a disconnected succession of green lanes marked as the 'Street Way' form a line with the sinuous character of a prehistoric trackway passing south of Great Wilbraham,[72] whence the line is taken up (TL 606633) by a metalled lane to St. Wendred's Well, in Exning (Suff.), and is later continued by a minor road (TL 632660) to the south end of Snailwell village and then further to the south-west corner of Chippenham Park (TL 660684) and beyond (TL 664686). The line from there to Badlingham, where it crossed the river Kennett (county boundary), is uncertain.[73]

The Northern Branch of the Icknield Way (route D, Bran Ditch via Whittlesford Bridge to Worsted Lodge)

Suggested as the main branch of the Icknield Way, it is held to diverge from the southern branch east of the crossing of the Bran Ditch and then curve north-eastwards across Thriplow Heath aligned on a barrow 500 metres north-west of Chrishall Grange. Thence it is indicated by a parish boundary which brings it to the present Royston–Newmarket road (TL 447451) which marks the course almost to Whittlesford bridge. A parish boundary, partly coinciding with the present road, marks the line to the river Cam, beyond which it is marked by the modern road as far as the north end of the Brent Ditch, from which the road through Babraham village takes it to Worsted Lodge.[74]

Barton via Comberton to Toft (route E)

It is generally accepted that a route ran from the junction of the bridle-path Deadman's Way with the Barton Road at least as far as Toft and possibly beyond to Ermine Street.[75] There is no definite evidence for its use in the Roman period, although the close association of Roman remains with the proposed line between Barton and Toft suggests that an earlier route continued to be used in Roman times.[76] The evidence for the course of the road beyond Toft is very doubtful.[77]

The Hardwick Way to the Portway (route F)

A vanished track which led from the Cambridge–Wimpole road near Deadman's Hill, Barton, to Hardwick was once known as the Hardwick way. Crossing Barton and Comberton fields it is suggested that it joined the Portway, which may have been a link between the valley of the Cam and Ermine Street by Hardwick. It was largely obliterated by inclosures in the 19th century, although some paths and lanes near Hardwick still bear the name. Its course cannot be traced west of Hardwick.[78]

[72] Cf. O.S. Map 1″, sheet 135 (1954 edn.): TL 535557 to 601629.

[73] The route described by Fox was not, according to Margaret Spufford, 'Street and Ditch Ways in SE. Cambs.', *Proc. C.A.S.* lix (1966), 129–31, the principal route to the Kennett: estate records indicate that the Street Way, also called South Street, crossed the S. end of Chippenham Park and reached the Kennett at the site of the bridge on the modern Newmarket–Thetford road, and that the Ditch Way was not the same as the Street Way, as assumed in *P.N. Cambs.* (E.P.N.S.), 30, but ran roughly parallel a little further S.

[74] Fox, *Arch. Camb. Region*, 145 and map D.

[75] Ibid. 169–70; Babington, *Ancient Cambs.* 49–50; Walker, in *Proc. C.A.S.* xiv. 169–71.

[76] The suggestion of Walker, in *Proc. C.A.S.* xiv. 170,

that until c. 1820 the main Barton–Toft road ran south of Comberton church is not borne out: *V.C.H. Cambs.* v. 175–6.

[77] Both Babington and Fox are uncertain about the continuation W. of Toft. Walker suggests that the route is marked by a path from Toft church to Kingston and thence by minor roads via Bourn to Caxton on Ermine Street, and that it was Romanized as far as Comberton or Caldecote.

[78] O.S. Map 1″, sheet 51 (1836 edn.), also showing a track from Childerley Gate to Hardwick, possibly connecting with the ridgeway (route B) from Madingley Hill to Eltisley: Fox, *Arch. Camb. Region*, 154, 171–2; cf. Babington, *Ancient Cambs.* 49–50; Walker, in *Proc. C.A.S.* xiv. 172.

Worts' Causeway to the Fleam Dyke (route G)

The section called Worts' Causeway, east of Red Cross, of the road from Cambridge to Worsted Lodge (Wool Street) aligns with the road along the parish boundary between West Wratting and Great Wilbraham, which has already been suggested as part of the Icknield Way, and together with the road west of Red Cross through Trumpington and Grantchester it may represent a western extension of a pre-Roman route, developed in Roman times, along the Stour valley through Great Thurlow (Suff.) and Weston Colville.[79]

Other Roads in the Cambridge Area

Few of the remaining routes which have been suggested have much evidence in their favour, although none can be ruled out until definitive investigations, including excavations, have been undertaken. The line of the present road from Royston on Ermine Street to Trumpington may go back to pre-Roman times, while a short road between Cambridge and Dam Hill, on the line of the medieval Milne Street, has also been suggested.[80]

A major pre-Roman road along the Cam valley, from Great Chesterford (Essex) to Trumpington, may have formed links between adjacent settlements rather than a continuous through route. A prehistoric ridgeway may have left the Icknield Way at Ickleton Granges (TL 461417) on the line of the road to Strethall (Essex) and continued to Ring Hill, in Littlebury (Essex), by what was known later as Walden Way.[81]

West of Cambridge there may have been a summer route from Bourn to Gamlingay, extending the Barton–Toft line (route E).[82] In the south-east a route skirting the edge of the forest zone parallel to the Icknield Way has been suggested, two branches originating in the Cam valley joining at Linton and running as a common way by Balsham, Stetchworth, and Cheveley to join the Icknield Way near Cavenham (Suff.). A dry-land route to settlements on the fen edge seems likely. Fox believed such a route to be medieval but with probably prehistoric origins.[83]

Fox's general observations on the relationship between roads and settlements during the Roman period bear repetition: 'while towns and settlements not infrequently occur at road junctions, the occupied areas as a whole bear little direct relation to the main Roman roads'.[84] The Roman roads proper were through-roads connecting major centres. Few settlements developed alongside them although crossroads were likely places for occupation. The pre-Roman farms and their Roman successors were linked by tracks and droves, many of which probably improved greatly in Roman times, a development detectable almost only through aerial photographs. Such routes linked the many small Roman settlements with the main Roman highways and with the old ridgeways that remained in use, such as the Icknield Way or the Eltisley ridgeway.

Appendix: Milestones and Other Inscriptions

Two Roman milestones, both of limestone and oval in section, were found in 1812 *c.* 5 km. beyond Cambridge beside the road to Godmanchester. One has a primary

[79] Fox, *Arch. Camb. Region*, 169; cf. Fox and Palmer in *Proc. C.A.S.* xxiv. 33. The possibility of a link between Worts' Causeway and the N. boundary of W. Wratting is strengthened by air photographs in the area of Hills and Rectory farms: R.C.H.M. *City of Camb.* i. 4.

[80] Fox, *Arch. Camb. Region*, 172; cf. Walker, in *Proc. C.A.S.* xv (1911), 192–6, recording a paved way at the W. end of Latham Road.

[81] Fox, *Arch. Camb. Region*, 145 n. 2 and maps D and III, 152.

[82] Ibid. 152 and map V. Fox believed that Eltisley was the nodal point in a network of pre-Roman routes, and that a hillside way connected Tadlow, Croydon, Orwell, and Haslingfield or Harston. A similar route may have linked Eversden, Harlton, and Haslingfield.

[83] Fox, *Arch. Camb. Region*, 153–5. Babington, *Ancient Cambs.* 80–1, suggested a prehistoric route into the S. fens from Camb. via Histon, Rampton, Belsar's Hill, and Haddenham to Witcham.

[84] Fox, *Arch. Camb. Region*, 219.

text only lightly incised: [I]MP(ERATORI) [CAES(ARI)] | FLA(VIO) VAL(ERIO) | C[O]NSTAN-TINO | PIO NOB(ILISSIMO) CAES(ARI) | DIVI | [CONST]ANTI | A[U]G(USTI) P[II | FILIO]. A secondary text has been more deeply incised: IMP(ERATORI) CAES(ARI) | FLAVI(O) | V(A)LE(RIO) | CONST|ANTI|NO PIO| NOB(ILISSIMO) CA|ES(ARI) [...]. The date of both texts is A.D. 306–7, when Constantine I was still Caesar, and the milestone is one of a series recording a renovation of the roads in the province when the authority of the

INSCRIPTIONS ON THE MILESTONES
FROM THE GODMANCHESTER ROAD

central imperial powers was re-established by Constantius I Chlorus (A.D. 296–306) after the separatist regime of Carausius and Allectus (286–96) had been defeated.

The second milestone has a primary text of which ...R... | AUG(USTUS) and a secondary of which [NOB]ILISSI|MUS CAESAR have been read.[85]

Otherwise the only inscription on stone from the county came from the settlement at Flaggrass, March (TL 434985).[86] The stone has been lost and no record of the text appears to survive.

SETTLEMENTS

The Pattern of Settlement

BEFORE the Roman conquest Cambridgeshire settlements of the Iron Age were placed mainly on the valley gravels in the south and on the well-drained chalk areas, usually near a water-course. The heavier claylands and most of the fenlands were avoided.

[85] R. G. Collingwood and R. P. Wright, *Roman Inscr. of Britain*, i, nos. 2236–7; both milestones are in Camb. Mus. For the shelly oolite used see J. P. Sedgley, *Roman*

Milestones of Brit. (B.A.R. 18, 1975), p. 24 nos. 22–3.
[86] *Roman Fenland*, 221.

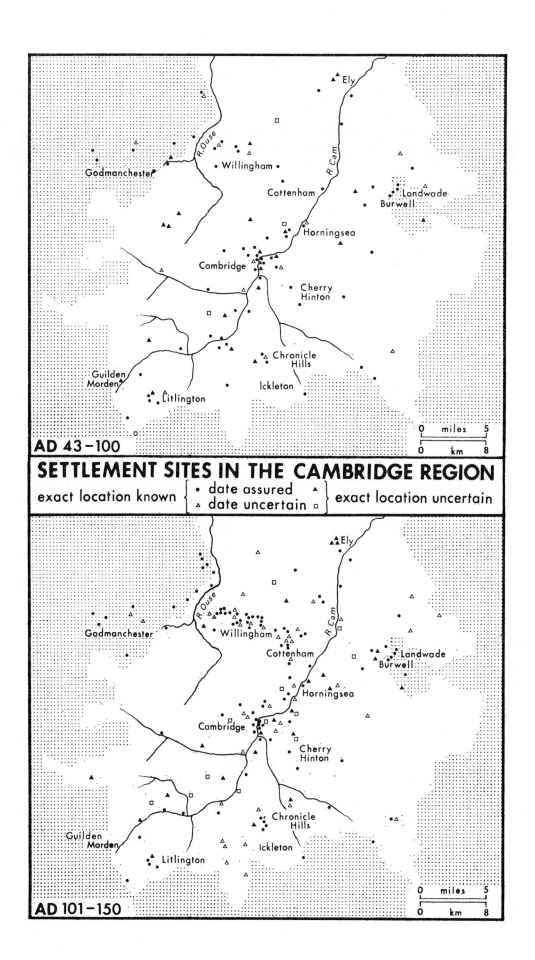

AD 43–100

SETTLEMENT SITES IN THE CAMBRIDGE REGION

exact location known { • date assured ▲
△ date uncertain □ } exact location uncertain

AD 101–150

The Roman conquest did not immediately alter the pattern.[1] Before the Flavian period (A.D. 70–96) the impact of Roman rule in the area appears to have been slight and there is no discernible increase of inhabited settlements: certainly the Boudiccan rebellion (A.D. 61) did not arrest any rapid Roman development in the area.[2] Some immigration into the area during the early Roman period has been suggested on various grounds, and punitive measures by the Romans in the immediate aftermath of the Boudiccan rising may have led to an increase in the amount of unoccupied land.[3] When more conciliatory policies were being followed the Roman authorities might well have introduced settlers from the adjacent continental mainland, a practice that was certainly adopted in other frontier areas of the Empire.

During the 2nd century there was almost everywhere an increase in both the density and the extent of settlement, reaching a peak during the second half of that century. The expansion is most marked in the fenlands, where previously settlement had been sporadic and had perhaps been linked with the salt extraction carried on in the north fenlands during the 1st century.[4] During the earlier 2nd century there was a large-scale colonization of the north fenlands, reflected in the numerous settlements with associated droves and waterways, whose beginnings are dated to the reigns of Hadrian (A.D. 117–38) and Antoninus Pius (138–61). A parallel expansion in the south fenlands may have started earlier in the same century.[5] Nor were other areas unaffected. Although the development of the fenlands, requiring extensive drainage works, stemmed from official action it is matched in form by an increase of settlement on areas away from the fen edge. The increase of settlement on fenland gravels, as in the vicinity of Cottenham and Willingham, was part of a general growth made possible by the drier conditions prevailing at the fen edge. Moreover people may have moved towards such areas because of pressure in the more upland gravel zones. Finally a rapidly expanding rural population may be the background to the growth of Cambridge, meeting the need for an economic and administrative centre.

Continuity from an earlier period suggests that the new settlers of the 2nd century were of native origin, although not necessarily from the areas immediately adjacent to the newly developed lands. The absence of regular over-all planning seems to rule out Roman veteran settlements, which were often accompanied by the dramatic imposition of a grid pattern with regular allotments marked out within the blocks of centuriated land (*ager centuriatus*), although individual settlers from such backgrounds may have received a land gratuity in the fenlands. Only the Roman government is likely to have initiated the drainage schemes, the roads, and boundary droves, which

---

[1] Cf. Fox, *Arch. Camb. Region*, 220. Fox's remark (p. 231) that 'what little we know of Romano–British agricultural settlements . . . suggests that they were essentially primitive communities of Early Iron Age peasants with but a slight veneer of Roman civilization' underestimates the impact of Roman rule and ignores the possibility of immigration, while his contrast between the early Romanization of the south and the retarded north cannot now be maintained.

[2] A similar continuity in settlement between Belgic and Roman has been observed in the valley of the Great Ouse: H. J. M. Green, in *Arch. News Letter*, vol. 5, no. 2 (1954), 29–32.

[3] The barrows have been considered as evidence for settlers from the Low Countries, although it is equally likely that they continue a local pre-Roman tradition: G. C. Dunning and R. F. Jessup, in *Antiquity*, x (1936), 37–49; Jessup, in *Jnl. Brit. Arch. Assoc.* 3rd ser. xxii (1959), 1. Early examples of the aisled house at Cherry Hinton and Landwade may also point to immigrants. It is

not clear whether the type of house had developed in Britain before the Roman conquest or was introduced afterwards: S. Applebaum, 'Roman Britain', *Agrarian Hist. of Eng. and Wales*, i (2), ed. H. P. R. Finberg (1972), 18. Salway, in *Roman Fenland*, 1, appears to discount the impact of immigrants and stresses, rightly it seems, that the essential distinctions by the 2nd cent. were those of social class rather than origin.

[4] The location of Salinae of the Catuvellauni near the Wash, which may be an error of co-ordination for the location at Droitwich (Worcs.), is adduced by Hallam, in *Roman Fenland*, 74, as showing that the earliest fenland colonists came from that people, enjoying an expansion of territory through a costly Roman allegiance during the Boudiccan rising. Icenian coins, however, are known in the fens, notably at March and Wisbech: Allen, in *Britannia*, i. 19.

[5] Not before *c.* A.D. 100 if Hartley's dating of the Car Dyke is an indication: *Roman Fenland*, 9.

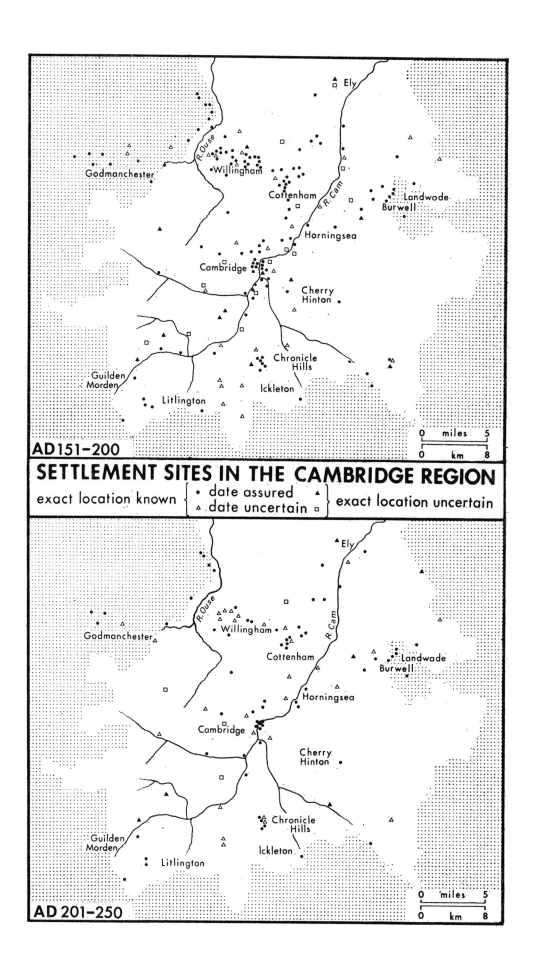

AD151-200

SETTLEMENT SITES IN THE CAMBRIDGE REGION

exact location known { • date assured ▲ } exact location uncertain
{ △ date uncertain □ }

AD 201-250

0 miles 5
0 km 8

had to be completed before the land could be settled. It is not inconceivable that the expansion of colonization that probably began under Trajan (A.D. 98–117) was given further impetus by the emperor Hadrian's visit to the province in 122.[6] In the Lincolnshire fenlands a fourfold increase in population between the mid 1st century and the late 2nd has been suggested with a density exceeding two-thirds of the Domesday level. The same may hold good also for the Cambridgeshire fenlands, but the further idea that the increase was fed by immigration[7] is not supported by firm evidence.

Freshwater flooding had a profound effect on the pattern of settlement in the fens and fen margins during the Roman period. Roman settlements in the south margins of the fen lay outside the limits of the peat deposits, which appear to have defined the lowest level at which settlement during the 2nd century was considered possible.[8] Many of the Roman settlements on the fen edges have gaps in their sequences of pottery that have been taken as evidence for an interruption of occupation during the period c. 230–c. 270. They lie close to the fen edge, while settlements occupied throughout the 3rd century lie further from the edge of the peat, an indication that it was flooding at the fen margin that caused the abandonment of settlements. The meandering course of the Old West River east of its junction with the Car Dyke indicates a breach caused by flooding in a Roman watercourse between Waterbeach and the Ouse at Earith made up of the Car Dyke or Old Tillage and straight stretches of the Old West River. The breach was the consequence of a large inundation in the second quarter of the 3rd century, its extent marked by the relative absence of pottery between Willingham West Fen and Stretham.[9] There were similar troubles elsewhere in the fenlands, notably in the north where settlements towards the fen edges suffered badly from flooding in the late 2nd century and later, although settlements on the higher siltlands nearer the sea continue to be occupied in spite of some inundation.[10]

In south Cambridgeshire the density of settlement decreased markedly in the earlier 3rd century, did not begin to recover until late in the same century, and did not reach the level of the late 2nd century. In Cambridge there are signs that the number of occupied houses had decreased and that some plots had become semi-derelict. The effects of the 3rd-century troubles of the Roman Empire, including the emergence of a separatist Gallic empire in A.D. 258, may have been especially severe on the Cambridgeshire region where increased prosperity depended on large-scale drainage works. The administration necessary to maintain such a large system may have failed at a time when flooding was particularly serious. Local self-help was perhaps undermined by political and administrative changes made by the Severan emperors in the early 3rd century (193–217),[11] and new arrangements for supplying the northern army from the fenlands, which may have been introduced by Severus, possibly curtailed economic development in the area.[12]

The two milestones from Girton, one dated to A.D. 306–7, may indicate how the

---

[6] Noted in later historical tradition for the order to build the wall in the north; the phrase 'multa correxit' in the imperial biography remains enigmatic.

[7] Hallam, in *Roman Fenland*, 71–4.

[8] John Bromwich, in *Roman Fenland*, 114–26; he observed the remarkable floods of March 1947 and noted that their limits coincided with the peat and peaty soil charted by the Geological Survey.

[9] Clark, in *Antiq. Jnl.* xxix. 145–63; Hartley, in *Roman Fenland*, 126.

[10] Cf. *Roman Fenland*, 230–3, 244–5, 247–8. Evidence of 3rd-cent. occupation is absent at Golden Lion inn, Stonea (TL 460934), Grandford House, March (TL 393996), and Coldham Clamp, Elm (TF 448027): Bromwich, in *Roman Fenland*, 120–1. In Lincs. about one-fifth

of the Hadrianic sites had ceased to be occupied by the end of the 3rd cent.

[11] Salway, in *Roman Fenland*, 10, 16, 20 n. 26, suggests that most of the reclaimed fenlands were part of the imperial estate; that the manner in which on his father's death Caracalla wound up the ambitious schemes of Septimius Severus (193–211) for northern conquest indicates indifference to local issues; and that local measures against flooding may have been hindered by the confiscation of the estates of Clodius Albinus' supporters and, if the Fen Causeway was the boundary between Britannia Superior and Inferior, by a division under Septimius or soon after between two provincial administrations.

[12] Salway, in *Roman Fenland*, 13; cf. Rivet, in *The Roman Villa in Britain*, ed. Rivet (1969), 200–1.

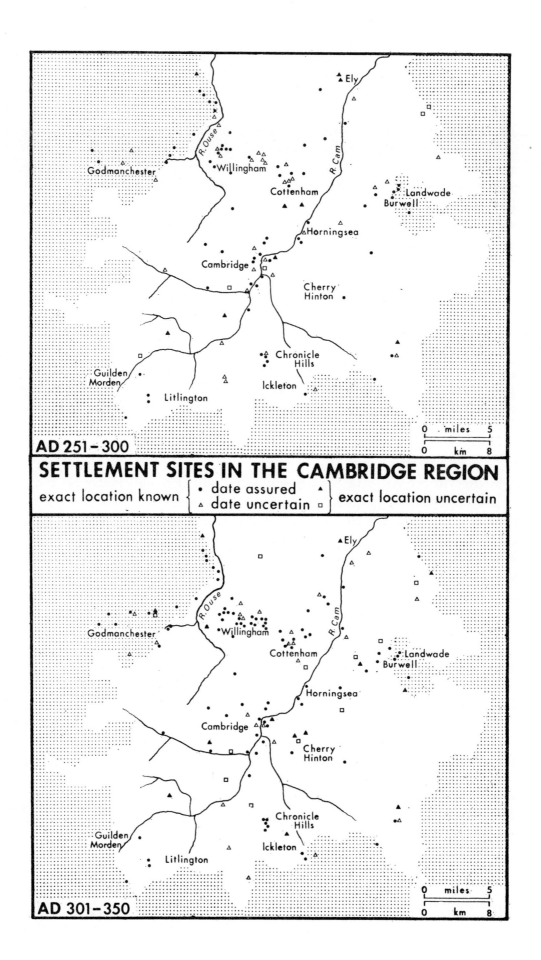

SETTLEMENT SITES IN THE CAMBRIDGE REGION

exact location known { • date assured ▲ } exact location uncertain
{ △ date uncertain ▫ }

AD 251–300

AD 301–350

0 miles 5
0 km 8

34

area shared in a general reconstruction of the province usually associated with the rule of Constantius I Chlorus (296–306).[13] It is uncertain how much attention was paid to the area by the separatist regimes of Carausius (286–93) and Allectus (293–6). Carausius, who came from the Menapii dwelling near the mouth of the Rhine, may conceivably have sought to revive the fenlands by introducing new settlers from his homeland, but is unlikely to have had opportunity during his brief reign to initiate such a major scheme.[14] Against the background of a climate that was becoming less favourable the reoccupation of sites in the south fenlands did not extend to those located at the lowest levels. An increase in the number of corn-drying ovens may reflect difficulties caused by damper conditions. The recovery is apparent in south Cambridgeshire also. Material remains in the villas suggest an improved economy, perhaps the result of private wealth introduced from Gaul and Germany, which were much less secure from barbarian attack.[15] The nature of the reconstruction is far from clear and presumably varied from area to area. Some of the fenlands may have been classed by the imperial authorities as 'vacant lands' (*agri deserti*), for which leases were offered at concessionary rates to attract new settlers or at least to tempt local landowners to accept new lands with their accompanying tax liabilities. Such measures may be partly responsible for a consolidation of the larger settlements compared with the somewhat more scattered pattern evident during the first period of prosperity in the late 2nd century.[16]

During the late 4th century there appears to have been a withdrawal of settlement from the fen edge, which, although not on a scale like that of the 3rd century, was probably caused by increasing waterlogging. In some parts of the fenlands the means to maintain drainage and flood protection were still available and occupation continued into the early 5th century, but the Roman pattern of occupation appears to have ceased at most sites by the middle of that century.[17] In the south Cambridge was walled by the mid 4th century but the defences were apparently not well maintained and may have been erected to meet a short-lived threat. The density of Roman settlement appears to have fallen away sharply in the late 4th century, although in some places occupation continued into the early 5th.

A decline of Roman settlement indicated by the distribution of identifiable Roman remains of the late 4th and early 5th centuries may have been counterbalanced by the arrival of Germanic settlers long before the Roman administration ceased to control the area. Their presence is attested by early Saxon cemeteries in East Anglia, and perhaps elsewhere by the occurrence of the so-called 'Romano-Saxon ware'. The status of the newcomers is not clear but they may have been soldiers introduced to protect imperial lands in the fens. If many of the long-established settlers in the area were, as has been suggested, of Germanic extraction, obstacles to assimilation were fewer.[18]

A sample of 322 sites in south Cambridgeshire reveals evidence of occupation during eight periods. The numbers of sites occupied in different periods indicate changes in the density of settlement. The rapid expansion of the 2nd century is clear, an expansion perhaps due partly to immigration. The peak in the late Antonine period represents only a small increment over the early 2nd century. The earlier 3rd century shows the

---

[13] See p. 4.
[14] Hallam, in *Roman Fenland*, 75; but cf. Salway, ibid. 16.
[15] Salway, ibid. 17.　　　　　　　　　　[16] Ibid.
[17] Bromwich, ibid. 122; cf. Salway, ibid. 18, suggesting that the necessary drainage maintenance ceased with the departure of the Roman officials, whereas Hallam, ibid.

47, cites evidence for late occupation, apparent continuities between Roman and Anglo-Saxon settlement layout, and re-use of Roman waterways.
[18] On the Saxon cemeteries see Lethbridge, in *V.C.H. Cambs.* i. 310–20, based on Fox, *Arch. Camb. Region*, 241–64; on 'Roman-Saxon' pottery J. N. L. Myres, *Anglo-Saxon Pottery and the Settlement of Eng.* (1969), *passim*.

decline to levels of the 1st century. The recovery in the late 3rd and early 4th century probably reflects the return to more stable conditions under Diocletian and Constantine but the levels of the 2nd century were not attained. Only a slight decline is shown before the end of the 4th century, while the dramatic decline in the early 5th century

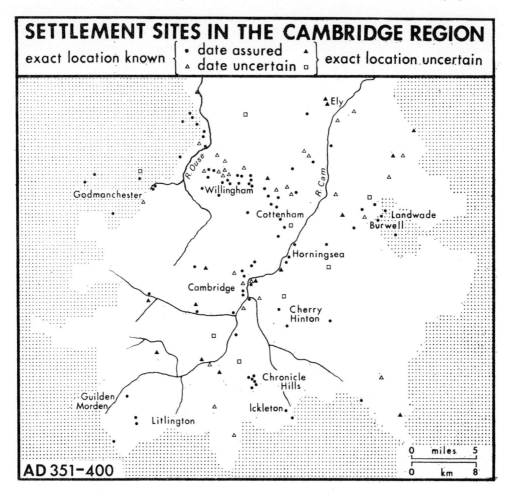

is perhaps a distortion because of the difficulty of dating Roman objects to that period, while settlements with Anglo-Saxon remains have been excluded. Nevertheless the sample shows a sharp decline in Roman settlements.

Period of occupation	Number of sites
A.D. 43–100	99
100–150	170
150–200	184
200–250	99
250–300	108
300–350	139
350–400	125
400–450	9

Categories and Types of Settlement

It is unlikely that Cambridge ever attained the status of a city during the Roman period, yet there is no doubt that, like the 'small towns' of Godmanchester (Hunts.) and Great Chesterford (Essex), it served as the urban focus for a surrounding area that is unlikely to have been closely defined for juridical or administrative purposes. South

Cambridgeshire was probably divided between at least three adjacent urban centres, Cambridge, Godmanchester, and Great Chesterford.[19] In the north the nearer part of the Ouse Valley doubtless looked towards Godmanchester, while Cambridge dominated the south of the county at least for several miles around. The distribution of pottery suggests that in the north-east the chalkland skirt to the fenlands also had links with

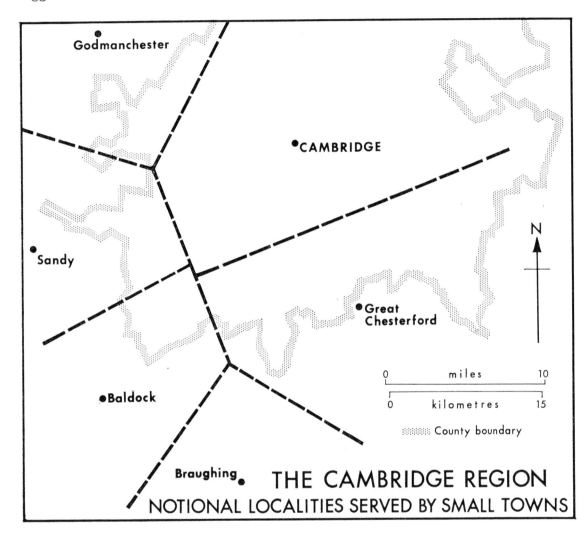

Godmanchester

•CAMBRIDGE

N

•Sandy

•Great
Chesterford

0   miles   10

0   kilometres   15

County boundary

Braughing• THE CAMBRIDGE REGION

•Baldock

NOTIONAL LOCALITIES SERVED BY SMALL TOWNS

Cambridge. In the south the Cam valley above Whittlesford, along with the chalk and boulder claylands of the extreme south and south-east, looked towards Great Chesterford. The far west may have looked towards Sandy (Beds.), and the south-west to Baldock (Herts.).[20] If the fenlands were part of an imperial estate the economy of the area may have been artificially ordered, although its natural links are likely to have been with settlements in the Nene Valley.

It may be assumed that the above centres served their localities as the first resort for more specialized goods and services, even though different areas may have been linked juridically and administratively with more remote centres such as Camulodunum (Colchester), Verulamium (St. Albans), and Venta Icenorum (Caister by Norwich). If the 'small town' was the highest level of settlement which existed in the county, it is likely that the more remote places, including also the provincial capital Londinium, were the sources of the most expensive goods that reached the area, high-quality

[19] I. Hodder, in *Small Towns of Roman Britain* (B.A.R. 15, 1975), 67–73.

[20] On Baldock see *Nature*, ccxix (1958), 435–6; *Britannia*, iv (1973), 298.

metalwork and jet objects being particular examples. Although the gathering of Roman taxes and local dues was controlled from outside the region the small towns are likely to have served as collection and distribution centres.

Notwithstanding the fact that many Roman titles are known for small settlements below the rank of city, in default of any written record one can only resort to descriptive categories which may in some instances be dangerously anachronistic. Of two types of settlement next below the level of small town one is an agglomerated unit which may be called village or hamlet according to its size. After A.D. 120 such settlements were more common than individual farms in the north fenlands: others existed in the south fenlands and elsewhere, although they were perhaps not so widespread in the rest of the county.[21] They were probably self-sufficient, with most domestic utensils being made from wood and bone. The characteristic rectangular dwelling was built of materials which were available locally, including thatch for roofs, clay for walls, and light timber for wattle.

The second type of settlement below the level of the small town was the villa estate, a form which could also incorporate a settlement of the village or hamlet type. As yet there is no definite evidence from south Cambridgeshire for villages independent of villa estates, which might represent communities of genuine freeholders. Like the villages of the fenlands, villa estates were largely self-sufficient for most daily needs, although a period of prosperity might lead to acquisitions of goods from further afield. As time passed there seems to have been a tendency for both villa estates and villages to increase in size, presumably at the expense of their neighbourhood rivals.[22]

The smallest type of settlement was the single farm, held freely or by a tenant (*colonus*) as part of a large domain, either private or imperial. Single farms are likely to have had even fewer external contracts than villages or villas, being able to participate in market exchange at only the most local level.

In the physical layout of individual settlements, determined partly by local conditions and partly by social and functional considerations, it has been possible to recognize two quite clearly defined types, the Wyboston type consisting of irregular small plots arranged relatively haphazardly in what has been called a 'native' fashion, and the St. Ives type, which has regular rectilinear plots of a 'Roman' type.[23] The former has a demonstrably pre-Roman origin. Both types are found in the fens and in other parts of the county, in some instances closely juxtaposed. In the fens the Wyboston type is characterized by ditched droves which are absent or at most very few in the St. Ives type, leading to dwellings surrounded by double ditches. The space between the inner and outer ditch was used probably for the overnight stockading of beasts collected from daily pasture, the entrance from the drove being closed by a gate or movable fence. Only wintering stock could probably be corralled in this fashion, the larger herd of the summer requiring bigger enclosures in or close to the pastures. Isolated enclosures approached by droves, or with droves pointing towards them, may be remains of such summer stockades, the finds from which probably belonged to the seasonal shacks of herdsmen. In some places it appears that a settlement of the St. Ives type superseded one of the Wyboston type, perhaps representing a reorientation of the economy, including a change of ownership.[24]

The persistence, and in some places the expansion, of a pre-Roman field pattern in

[21] Hallam, in *Roman Fenland*, 51–4.
[22] Alterations in the late period at Arbury Road Site II: Alexander, Excavation Rep. 1968; interpreted, though the evidence is slight, as indicating social change or even a peasants' revolt by Applebaum, in *Agrarian Hist.* i (2), 223 sqq.

[23] Applebaum, in *Agrarian Hist.* i (2), 12–14. Others prefer to retain the term 'Celtic' fields for the native form.
[24] Ibid. 31.

the Roman period has been cited as clear evidence for a substantial continuity in rural population and the Roman authorities' recognition of pre-Roman tenurial arrangements, although as time passed the growth of large private estates and occasional confiscation may have severely disrupted traditional patterns of landholding. A custom of subdividing family holdings may have contributed to the growth of villages in the fenlands;[25] if so, and if the developed fenlands were imperial property, tenants disposed of leases through testament with official sanction.

It has been suggested that in the fenlands the standard size of holding was around 45 hectares or close to the well-known Roman *centuria* of 200 *iugera* (approx. 49 hectares).[26] Deductions about social arrangements have often begun with a study of house plans. The aisled house which occurs from the early Roman period has been designated as evidence for a 'self-contained homestead', with people and animals occupying the same building.[27]

Cambridge

Through most if not all of the Roman period the settlement which lies beneath the northern part of modern Cambridge played an important role in the life of the region.[28] Roman Cambridge lay on the north bank of the Cam on a low promontory close to a ford, the district now called Castle Hill or Castle End, consisting of Gault capped with Lower Chalk which has a shallow mantle of Pleistocene sands and gravels. A Belgic settlement of the late 1st century B.C. is attested by hut enclosures. Two enclosures found in Ridgeon's Gardens with diameters of *c.* 23 metres were oval and contained huts with chalk and gravel floors. When the settlement was abandoned at the Roman conquest it had passed through three structural phases.[29]

The earliest Roman features belong to the period between the conquest and the beginning of the Flavian period. Two rectilinear ditched enclosures on the site of Shire Hall have been interpreted as evidence for a military occupation. A palisade trench which has been traced for 28 metres on a north–south line in Ridgeon's Gardens is of the mid 1st century A.D. Measuring 1 metre wide with vertical sides and 1.8 deep it had held a row of posts later withdrawn before the ditch was deliberately filled. An entrance through the palisade was later blocked by a fence.[30]

During the last quarter of the 1st century the palisade was replaced by an enclosure aligned parallel to the Godmanchester road, with a cobbled area fronting the road. The south-east side was at least 70 metres long, marked by a V-shaped ditch 3.6 metres wide and 1.5 metres deep with a rounded butt end at an entrance, and has been interpreted as the ditch of a Roman fort of the Flavian period. No trace remained of the rampart, and inside the fort only a cobbled court and a hearth were discovered. The ditch was recut at least once before the end of the Flavian period and from the amount

[25] Ibid. 48.   [26] Hallam, in *Roman Fenland*, 66–7.

[27] Applebaum, in *Agrarian Hist.* i (2), 45, citing the aisled house at Cherry Hinton; see above, p. 31 n. 3. Aisled buildings often found as subsidiary elements in villa complexes may have housed farm workers. Applebaum believed that the early aisled house may have been that of the king or chief. Evidence from the Landwade villa in Exning (Suff.) suggests the survival of a pre-Roman social order in a house altered by Roman improvements: Salway, in *Roman Fenland*, 235. At Ickleton (below, p. 46) the basilican building may represent a combination of basilican house and two-roomed farm dwelling, with one end cut off from the hall by a wall: cf. Applebaum, in *Agrarian Hist.* i (2), 126. The barn at Ickleton used for wintering stock had an aisled plan, with animals stalled between the columns; the aisle was narrow because used exclusively for animals.

[28] The meagre evidence registered in Fox, *Arch. Camb. Region*, 174–5, has been substantially increased through excavations by Dr. J. A. Alexander, who pending full publication in *Proc. C.A.S.* has given an interim summary in *Small Towns of Roman Britain* (B.A.R. 15, 1975) and has most generously made his results available for the present survey.

[29] The enclosure ditches in Ridgeon's Gardens, *c.* 3 metres wide and 2 metres deep, and a pond and gravel- and marl-pits yielded pottery, bronze and iron objects, and bones of cattle, sheep, and pigs. An early Roman road overlay an enclosure ditch east of Ridgeon's Gardens.

[30] Contemporary features found in Comet Place include ditches, two pits, and a possible latrine containing Claudian pottery.

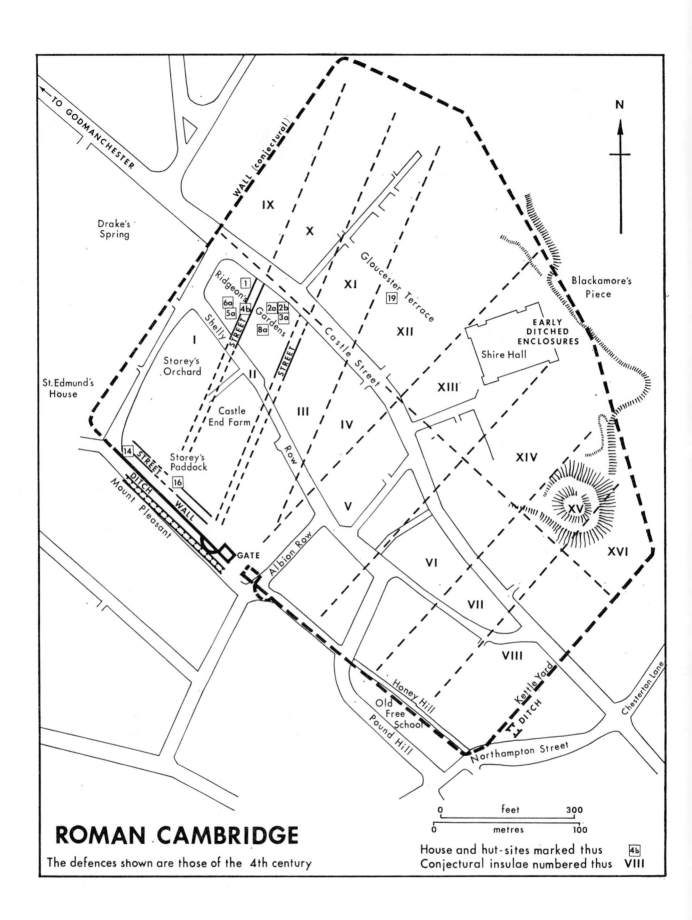

of silting seems to have remained in use into the 2nd century. Houses built north-west of the enclosure at that period did not approach within 100 metres, an isolation suggestive of continued military presence.[31] Whether the occupation was civilian or military the degree of regulation suggests that Cambridge had developed as an administrative centre before the end of the 1st century. That role may have been greatly enhanced by development of the fenlands in the early 2nd century.

In the 2nd century all existing structures were removed and the entire area of Ridgeon's Gardens was levelled. An earlier pond on the site was drained and streets of cambered gravel were laid at an angle to the main axis of the settlement, formed by the Godmanchester road. The insulae defined by the streets mark the beginning of the history of Roman Cambridge as an urban centre. The timber buildings so far excavated in the north-west end of the town do not suggest a highly Romanized community, even when it was enclosed by substantial stone walls in the 4th century.[32]

In insula I (Ridgeon's Gardens) among several timber buildings a rectangular house (hut 1) aligned on the street had daub walls, a cement floor and perhaps a tile roof, and a gravel yard enclosed by a gated fence. Two other houses (5a, 6a), one aligned on the Godmanchester road, ceased to be inhabited in the 3rd century but hut 1 remained in use into the 4th century. Elsewhere in the insula (Storey's Paddock) was a timber house (13) with a yard; it had been abandoned before the end of the 2nd century, while another area (Mount Pleasant) remained open until a timber house (14) was built in the late 2nd century. It had an earth floor on which were placed a succession of hearths, and was probably associated with a fenced and gated yard, beyond which were successive latrine and refuse pits.

Further south-east in an area (Ridgeon's Gardens) of insula II a rectangular hut (2a) with a chalk floor was built immediately after the street was built, and another (2b) was built with a gravel and marl floor in the mid 2nd century, to be replaced later by a rectangular house (3a) which contained a large hearth and had a yard outside. All three sites were replaced in the late 2nd century by an open yard (3) surfaced with gravel and chalk and associated with two clay-walled ovens. Beneath the floor, within the west boundary ditch, was a child burial.[33] The relatively high level of development in insulae I and II contrasts with insula XII (Gloucester Terrace, east of the Godmanchester road) which appears to have served as a refuse dump.[34]

During the 3rd century the substantial timber house (1) in insula I (Ridgeon's Gardens) continued to be occupied and its yard was resurfaced more than once. Other houses seem to have lain abandoned, with their sites used for dumping refuse.[35] The hearths and floor of the house (14) in insula I (Mount Pleasant) were periodically refurbished into the 4th century and the yard also remained in use. Pits[36] of the 3rd century in insula II (Ridgeon's Gardens and Storey's Paddock) attest also some

[31] The ditch as recut was 1·5 metres wide and 1·2 metres deep. Contemporary with the fort were pits, a latrine, and a well at least 4 metres deep containing brooches, the impression of an iron bowl or helmet, part of an articulated ox skeleton, and late-1st-cent. pottery. Also contemporary were a pit in Storey's Orchard and a timber hut (7) in Storey's Paddock.

[32] Finds of tesserae near St. Peter's church overlooking the river suggest that better appointed buildings may lie in the S. part of the Roman town; cf. similar development at Godmanchester: Green, in *Small Towns of Roman Britain*, 191–202.

[33] Part of a contemporary house (3b) was aligned to the cross street and remains of other 2nd-cent. houses (4, 9, 10) were recorded.

[34] Some 2nd-cent. pits are known and on the Shire Hall

site there may have been buildings. No structures have been excavated in insulae III–IV or IX–XII, and insulae XIII–XVI have not been excavated in a scientific fashion.

[35] Perhaps in an orderly fashion: caches of pottery were in well-dug pits, some of which may have been dug for marl.

[36] In the S. part of Ridgeon's Gardens a line of nine rectangular flat-bottomed pits c. 1 by 1·5 metre and 2 metres deep, dated to the 3rd cent., each contained two or three infant burials in a basket or rush mat. Six pits contained dogs, and one shoe-nails. Near by a circular 3rd-cent. well had staggered foot-holes and contained a horse's skeleton and many iron objects. Another well c. 1 metre square was timber-lined with foot-holes in one corner: J. Pullinger, in *Britannia*, vii (1976), 340–1.

continuing inhabitation although the surrounding area appears to have been quarried extensively for gravel. Elsewhere in insula II (Storey's Paddock) a new house (15) was built with a cement floor.[37]

Occupation in the town during the 4th century is divided into two phases by the construction of the defences. In insula I the earlier house (14) and its yard remained occupied until demolished to allow the building of the defences (Mount Pleasant). More gravel-digging is found in insula II (north end of Storey's Paddock) with abandoned pits later used for refuse until filled and levelled during the building of the walls and the accompanying intervallum road.[38]

In the mid 4th century the settlement was enclosed by a stone wall and a ditch. Part of the north-west wall was found at Drake's Spring and the ditch on the same side was found running at right angles to the Godmanchester road. The west corner probably lies beneath the entrance to St. Edmund's House.[39] Recent discoveries have demonstrated that, contrary to earlier belief, the north part of the south-west side does not correspond with the line of the present embankment, while its south continuation has been observed on the site of the old Lancasterian Free School.[40] The south-east ditch was sectioned at Honey Hill and is believed to continue north-east roughly on the line of Kettle Yard.[41] The location north-east of Castle Street is unknown although it certainly lay north-west of Chesterton Lane.[42] Some walling probably belonging to the north-east defences was noted on Blackamore's Piece[43] but the position of the east corner has yet to be located.

More recent excavations have furnished some details. The ditch at Honey Hill was 2·45 metres deep, 10·7 metres across with a flat bottom 3·35 metres broad, and had similar dimensions at Blackamore's Piece. At Honey Hill masonry probably from the wall had collapsed or been pitched into the ditch before much silt had accumulated. The south-west rampart was 9·30 metres wide at the base and was made of material from the ditch. In Mount Pleasant the stone wall was 2·75 metres thick laid in a foundation trench 0·6 metres deep, and was made of Northamptonshire limestone, clunch, flint, and bonding tiles, found as debris in the robbing trench. The wall and rampart (an unusual feature for the period) appear to have been contemporary. Inside the rampart a gravel road was laid down. The positions of the gates are inferred from the street plan, except for the south-west gate. Excavation there has revealed a single carriageway with semicircular projecting towers and a guard room recessed behind the wall which had a reduced thickness of 1·5 metres on either side of the gate.[44]

The building of the defences was accompanied by extensive building within the walls. The north-west cross street (Ridgeon's Gardens) was resurfaced and in insula I house (1) and its yard built in the 2nd century continued to be occupied, while the yard was resurfaced and given a new fence. A new square house (4b) was built of timber, with walls of wattle and daub plastered on the inside and a tile roof. A gravelled yard alongside contained a well-house covering a well more than 6·5 metres deep which later collapsed and was used as a rubbish tip. Of two other new houses one (5b) was aligned to the Roman Street and the other (6b) contained a hearth. Elsewhere in the same insula (Storey's Paddock) a timber house (16) was built at the same time as the

[37] Between Mount Pleasant and St. John's playing-field 3rd-cent. material has been found beyond the later walled area. Within the town no structure has been securely identified in insulae III–VIII or IX–XVI.

[38] No definite evidence for this phase is known for insulae III–XI or XIII–XVI.

[39] Downing Coll., Camb., Bowtell MSS. ii. 98–9, 175; Browne, in *Proc. C.A.S.* lxv (i), 17.

[40] Bowtell MSS. ii. 98–9.

[41] R.C.H.M. *City of Camb.* i. 8.

[42] Alexander proposes a line beneath the Norman motte and southern curtain wall of the castle.

[43] Bowtell MSS. ii. 162.

[44] The foundation trench was lined with gravel, then covered with chalk marl sealed by mortar on which the wall, which has been robbed throughout, was laid.

defences on a platform of limestone rubble, loam, and clay, with a floor of puddled marl, walls of daub, and a tile roof. The yard contained a hearth of flint and clay. After the house had been destroyed by fire two rubbish pits dug through the demolition rubble attest a continuing occupation. Near by a new house (17) was built on the intervallum road which had gone out of use when the other house (16) was destroyed. After the later house (17) was abandoned a loam developed over this derelict quarter. Near by in the same insula (Storey's Orchard) a house or yard with flint and clay surface was associated with several pits, one of which contained roof-tiles and red painted wall-plaster indicating a more substantial building in the vicinity.

In insula II (Ridgeon's Gardens) the yard (3) continued in use and at least one new house (8a) and perhaps a second (12) with a yard were built. Elsewhere gravel-pits (Shelly Row) and other pits (Castle End Farm and Albion Row) have been recorded. Several phases of 4th-century occupation in an area of insula XII (Gloucester Terrace) began with a yard floored with broken flint into which a marl-pit was later excavated before a period of desertion and dereliction. The building of a house (19) was accompanied by a yard similar to the earlier one and bounded by a drainage gully renewed at least three times. Later marl-pits were dug and an accumulation of soil indicates renewed dereliction.[45]

Across the river a small settlement grew on and near the firm gravel at St. Sepulchre's Hill, beginning in the 2nd century and continuing into the 4th. A small industrial quarter probably of the late 3rd or early 4th century is indicated by the pottery wasters at Jesus Lane. No trace of a bridge has been found, although a wooden causeway 4·30 metres below the modern surface of Bridge Street may, if it is of Roman origin, have connected the St. Sepulchre's settlement with a bridge or ford over the river.[46]

From the evidence recovered in the northern area it appears that Roman Cambridge came to an end during the earlier 5th century. There is no sign of any sudden catastrophe, and the impression gained is of a gradual abandonment as vegetation rapidly covered derelict buildings. Nevertheless it could still be recognized at the end of the 7th century[47] for what it had once been. There was perhaps no sudden decline in population, and as the town gradually shrunk to a bridgehead settlement the earlier population may have drifted away to a new pattern of villages established by the English settlers.

Villas

The numerous Roman villas with their mosaic floors and hypocaust heating systems represent the most familiar material legacy of Roman Britain. Cambridgeshire falls markedly short of other counties in the number and variety of villas found within its borders. Because no Cambridgeshire villa has been completely excavated, because the published record of excavations remains incomplete, because some published accounts were compiled many years ago, and because recent excavations have been undertaken with the urgency of rescuing the barest minimum, it is hard to relate the villa economy of the county to studies of other areas where circumstances are more propitious.[48]

Near Cambridge two villas have been identified at Arbury Road. On the south in an

---

[45] No structures were identified in insulae III–IV and no well-stratified remains in V–XI. The extent of occupation in the Castle Hill area is shown by pottery from Castle Yard, Shire Hall, Castle Street police sta., the old law courts, Kettle Yard, St. Peter's churchyard, and Pound Hill.

[46] Excavation by Mr. C. Partridge, not yet published.

See also Browne, in *Proc. C.A.S.* lxv (1), map 2 and pp. 18–22. Roman occupation from the 1st cent. in what became the Saxon town is known at Trinity Hall: ibid. p. 21 no. 34.

[47] *Bede's Eccl. Hist.* ed. B. Colgrave and R. A. B. Mynors (1969), 394–5.

[48] Cf. *The Roman Villa in Britain*, ed. Rivet.

area of more than 3 ha. around Humphreys Road and Fortescue Road (TL 451608) was found an L-shaped stone building containing three or four rooms, along with other remains including walls of neighbouring buildings, working floors, a pottery kiln, storage and refuse pits, and a cemetery of inhumations and cremations. Occupation appears to have begun c. A.D. 130 and continued beyond A.D. 400 on the evidence of a hoard of 17 coins near the footings of the south wall. The main building (TL 45126083) measured 8·6 by 5·3 metres with an annexe on the south measuring 4·05 by 2·95 metres. With footings of chalk blocks and mortar the walls were probably of timber coated outside with orange or brown and inside with white plaster. All rooms except the northernmost had mortar floors, and one had a hearth. The roof was of tile, and box-tiles indicate some heating system. The block was built, over earlier filled pits, in the 4th century and remained occupied until late in that century. The annexe had a similar character but with a design of red and white panels on the inside walls while the footings were pitched blocks of chalk with a rubble and mortar core and ashlar outer courses on the south and east. The annexe was roofed with ragstone slabs and had glazed windows, and was built after A.D. 330 on the evidence of a coin in a well partly covered by the annexe. Lined with oak planks descending in narrowing tiers, the well belonged to the 2nd century and had been filled with the rubble from a burnt timber building perhaps of c. A.D. 150 on a site west of the later stone block.[49] Nothing can be inferred of the social or economic life of the settlement. The residents evidently enjoyed a modest standard of personal comfort with the basic amenities of Roman life.

In the area of the King's Hedges estate a substantial settlement, selectively excavated, was occupied from Iron Age to Roman times.[50] On one site (II) occupation did not begin until the 1st century A.D. and several ditches contained debris from buildings over a period from the 1st to the 4th century. In the second occupation phase a rectangular building with aisles formed by square columns was constructed partly in stone. In the centre of the south wall was an entrance porch to which a road led from the south-east. Debris from the building included tesserae, floor-tiles, wall-plaster, flue-tiles, and limestone blocks re-used in a later building, some of which were carved (see below, p. 67). It appears that the building, which was destroyed by fire, was occupied in the 2nd and 3rd centuries. Its function remains obscure but the sculptured blocks may indicate a religious use. In the late 3rd or early 4th century the derelict building was adapted for use as a house with two suites of rooms flanking a large hall or court. Three or four of the rooms on the south were heated and had tessellated floors, plastered walls, and glazed windows. North of the tessellated court was a kitchen block. The debris of an associated well included blocks of carved limestone besides six human skulls.[51]

On the south skirt of the fenlands the villa at the Temple, Isleham (TL 631739), is attested by debris from the later earthwork, which included mosaic, painted plaster, and roof- and box-tiles, while a mosaic of red and grey tesserae measuring 3·65 by 4·00 metres lay near by along with a concrete floor.[52] Landwade villa (TL 612676), in Exning (Suff.), is just outside the county but is well recorded and may be typical of the

[49] W. H. C. Frend, in *Proc. C.A.S.* xlviii (1955), 10–43. For the coffin burials see below, p. 89. Chalk floors elsewhere on the site may mark timber buildings of the early phase. On the N. side of Montgomery Road a 4th-cent. building of ragstone and chalk, destroyed by fire, was replaced by a larger rectangular building in chalk differently aligned.

[50] See Plate VIA. Browne, in *Proc. C.A.S.* lxv (1), p. 12; cf. ibid. pp. 29–30 under map 12; Alexander, Excavation

Rep. 1967, 1968, 1969.

[51] Remains from other sites (IV, VI, VII) consisted largely of pits and enclosure ditches. On site I a pit contained Romano-Saxon pottery and more carved stone. On site VIII a Belgic and pre-Belgic settlement was superseded by a field system of the late 1st or early 2nd cent. A.D. For the sculpture blocks at site II see below, pp. 67–8.

[52] Salway, in *Roman Fenland*, 236.

area.[53] A mosaic south of a bath building suggests a substantial villa.[54] Timber huts of the Flavian period, revealed in recent excavations, were replaced probably in the early 2nd century by a timber barn-house 31·7 metres long with a nave 5·5 and an aisle 2·45 metres wide. In the late 2nd century the aisle wall was rebuilt in stone and a bath suite was inserted into the north-west end of the nave. In the course of a complete rebuilding in stone during the 3rd century the baths were modified and a dining room (*triclinium*) with semicircular mosaic was added to the south end, beyond which was another heated room. Occupation seems to have ended with an extensive fire in the early 4th century. At Biggin Farm, Fordham (TL 637683), pottery of the 2nd to the 4th century, accompanied by wall-plaster and roof- and flue-tiles, appears to indicate a villa.

While some sites are difficult to classify, for example the Roman building on the site of the later Burwell castle (TL 58726605), which has not been firmly established as a *villa rustica*,[55] the remains of the villa at Reach (TL 57266518) are in no way ambiguous.[56] The plan of the main residence belongs to the winged corridor type, comprising a rectangular block at least 40 metres long and 7·75 metres wide. There may have been a portico along the rear of the building. The wings project about 12·6 metres, with small apses in each of the front façades. A small bath suite projected from the south-west corner, and the heated main room at the centre of the rear range projected north-west beyond the main façade. Both corners of the rear range have projecting chambers in the fashion of wings.[57] The high quality of building and materials used throughout suggests that although many of the Cambridgeshire villas were small they may have been well designed and elegantly appointed.[58]

In south and west Cambridgeshire Roman villas form an important element in an almost unbroken line of settlements along the valley of the upper Cam and its tributaries. One settlement existed north of the confluence of the Cam and Bourn south of Grantchester. Remains of stone and timber buildings (TL 43205495) were noted (but not planned) during the First World War, and building debris included building stone, roof tiles, painted plaster and *opus signinum*. Refuse pits and a well 8·90 metres deep contained much debris and some charred oak beams that have been interpreted as part of a windlass. A stone column at Carter's Well, Grantchester (TL 431548), suggests that the building may have been a villa, linked with the extensive cropmark site at Cantelupe Farm, Haslingfield.[59]

Further west the villa at Comberton (TL 38455489) included a bath suite with rectangular rooms heated by a hypocaust with brick *pilae*. The walls (1·0 metre thick) were built of Ketton stone, chalk marl, and large flints. One room was hexagonal with sides 3·00 metres long and like several others contained painted walls. Among finds which included columns, lead pipes, pottery, a glass bottle, bone pins, and a bronze padlock the coins extended from Vespasian (69–79) to Gratian (375–83).[60] Among several villas in the valley of Cam or Rhee and its tributaries the 'houses' at Shepreth noted as containing floors of *opus signinum* and tile-floored 'passages' have yielded finds of white tesserae and painted plaster suggestive of more elegant buildings near

[53] *Proc. C.A.S.* xi (1907), 210; E. Greenfield, in *J.R.S.* xlix (1959), 128; l (1960), 228–9; cf. *Roman Fenland*, 235.

[54] Hughes, in *Proc. C.A.S.* xi (1907), 210. Three sections of the mosaic are in the Cambridge Museum.

[55] Roman remains in NE. Cambs., including numerous sites on the fen skirt, are described in R.C.H.M. *Cambs.* ii. For Burwell see Lethbridge, in *Proc. C.A.S.* xxxvi (1936), 121–3; R.C.H.M. *Cambs.* ii. 40–1.

[56] See Plate IVв. R.C.H.M. *Cambs.* ii. 88–9 and fig. 80.

[57] D. R. Wilson, in *Britannia*, v (1974), 258 and plate xxvi.

[58] Walls (0·5–0·8 metres thick, 0·6 in hypocaust) were well made of flint with brick quoins, the hypocaust had

brick *pilae*, and the main room in the SW. wing had flue-tiles in the corners and a lining of *opus signinum* in the apse. Wall-plaster painted in several colours bears floral motifs. Other finds include pottery, animal bones, iron hooks, and a piece of lead containing an iron bolt. Substantial Iron Age settlements are known near by at Church Hill (TL 56406536) and Devil's Ditch (TL 575656); from the latter come Roman pottery, tiles, and painted plaster: cf. R.C.H.M. *Cambs.* ii. 88.

[59] N. T. Porter, in *Proc. C.A.S.* xxii (1921), 124–6.

[60] *Gent. Mag.* n.s. viii (1842), 526; *Arch. Jnl.* vi (1849), 210; Fox, *Arch. Camb. Region*, 185.

by.[61] The building at Wimpole (TL 43335486) has been identified as part of a posting station (*mutatio*) rather than as a villa.[62] Further south, on 'Ashwell Street', the large 4th-century villa at Litlington with its walled cemetery (TL 313425) is ill recorded. The main building had at least thirty rooms arranged around a courtyard and occupied an area 150 by 90 metres. Appointments included a bath suite, a mosaic pavement, and a tessellated floor in another near-by building.[63] The villa at Chronicle Hills, Whittlesford (TL 452476), is evident from surface traces which have produced a collection of pottery, tiles, tesserae, wall-plaster, and window glass.[64] At Ickleton the corridor-type villa faced east and measured 29·65 by 20 metres. A building 17·0 by 7·3 metres was connected to the residence by a wall at the south-west angle, and there is a basilican aisled building measuring 25 by 12·5 metres. The walls there were of flint and clunch with tile quoins. The internal piers were capped with Ketton stone and the roof was of stone slabs. A coin of Hadrian (117–38) was found in the footings of the residence and coins of the 4th century have come from the other buildings.[65] The Roman residence at Church Field, Bartlow, may have belonged to the builders of the Bartlow Hills barrows (Essex), or more probably to their descendants or successors. The small building (13 by 14·6 metres) had a bath suite in the south part but elsewhere was not well appointed. Coins from a refuse pit attest occupation continuing into the later 4th century.[66]

A villa at Guilden Morden (TL 277405) may have been connected with the cemetery there in the fashion of the villa at Litlington. Its focus consists of a rectangular house and subdivided courtyard. Aerial photographs reveal that ditches of a rectangular enclosure were filled to allow construction of what was probably a stone barn. The original access to the main house was a causeway across the ditch on the east, replaced by a stone gatehouse when the barn was built. The main residence may have been timber-framed, except for the bath suite at the south end.[67] A possible villa at Dutter End, Gamlingay (TL 24555250), lies in an area of sparse settlement. The villa at Hoffer Brook Farm, Foxton (TL 41404985), consists of a rectangular house within an enclosure, with fields on the south. A possible villa at the Plantation, Great Shelford (TL 457539), has rectilinear fields on the north-west. Among a number of settlements along Wool Street south-east of Cambridge the villa at Copley Hill, Babraham (TL 50555325), is set within a courtyard which has subsidiary enclosures. Some long boundaries running east of the villa are like those sometimes interpreted as ranch boundaries. Similar long ditches have been observed near the possible villa at Allington Hill, Bottisham (TL 578588), which, like Copley Hill, includes chalklands suitable for sheep: a rectangular enclosure of nearly 1½ ha. south of the Street Way includes a number of subdivisions, the main one in the north-east corner, and at its centre has produced surface finds from a building including 3rd- and 4th-century pottery.[68]

[61] C.A.S. *Rep.* 46, p. lx; Babington, *Ancient Cambs.* 63–4. No account has yet been published of reputedly prolific recent excavations. An extensive system of rectilinear enclosures NE. of the villa probably represents fields of the estate, whose *villa rustica* shows clearly in aerial photographs.

[62] W. P. Westell, in *Trans. E. Herts. Arch. Soc.* ix (1937), 363; cf. R.C.H.M. *Cambs.* i, p. lix. Recent (unpublished) work near Wendy close to the junction of Ermine Street and the Cambridge–Wimpole road suggests a road station or substantial roadside settlement.

[63] A. J. Kempe, in *Archaeologia*, xxvi (1836), 76; *Arch. Jnl.* vi. 14–26; cf. Joan Liversidge, *Britain in the Roman Empire*, 260. Rectilinear enclosure seen east of the villa (TL 323427) on aerial photographs may represent the estate's fields.

[64] Collected by B. Beveridge, R.A.F., and stored in Camb. Mus.

[65] C. Roach Smith, in *Jnl. Brit. Arch. Assoc.* [1st ser.], iv (1849), 356–68.

[66] R. C. Neville, in *Arch. Jnl.* x (1853), 17–21; cf. R.C.H.M. *Essex*, i, p. xxi.

[67] See Plate IIIA. *J.R.S.* lxiii (1973), 245 and plate XVIII (2). See also Wilson, in *Britannia*, v. 254–5.

[68] See Plate IVA. Two roughly rectangular enclosures less than 0·2 ha. in area 400 metres SE. of Allington Hill were superseded by ditches linked by a single ditch to a broad ditch 1·1 km. long, and may be earlier Iron Age or Roman farmsteads replaced by pastures of a late Roman estate: see R.C.H.M. *Cambs.* ii. 12.

In the south-east quarter of the enclosure stood two or more timber aisled structures. Circular buildings in the north-west quarter were probably round houses.[69]

The Fenlands

Settlement in the south fenlands appears to be distributed in relation to the edges of the gravel and watercourses. The edge of the gravel was more often an attraction than the closeness of water, and the edge rather than the centre of the gravel was chosen apparently for its nearness to both the wetter and the drier ground. The alluvial and clay lands served as meadows producing hay, important for the cattle economy of the fenlands, while gravels provided year-round pasture besides supporting sheep and producing some cereals. Droves and lanes between the gravel and alluvial lands mark the seasonal movement of livestock. Excessive waterlogging of the meadow eventually forced changes on the Roman economy of the area.[70]

A classification of settlements in the Cambridgeshire fenlands, on the lines of that for Lincolnshire,[71] is not yet possible. The dominant characteristics of settlement layout not yet hitherto recognized may, however, be seen in the individual features of selected sites.

Beginning with the south fenlands and the fen edge, a zone geographically distinct from the north, the settlement at Fen Drayton (TL 336682) consists of a rectilinear enclosure with multiple ditches, with which are associated droves and a system of irregular fields.[72] Excavation of the settlement at Cold Harbour Farm, Over (TL 393698), revealed continuous occupation from the 1st century A.D., perhaps beginning before the conquest, and a pottery kiln of the 1st and early 2nd century.[73] In a mound at Elney Low Fen, Fen Drayton (TL 335703), a continuity of occupation in Iron Age, Roman, and Saxon periods was found, and a pre-Roman to Roman continuity was found at Further Way, Over (TL 392717), which comprises a group of contiguous enclosures limited by droves on the north-west and north-east.[74]

The settlement at West Fen central, Willingham (TL 396714),[75] comprised dispersed rectangular enclosures of different sizes divided by a drove and ditch from the next settlement to the north at West Fen north-east, Willingham (TL 398719). The former site had droves linking gravel land to the wetter alluvial zone. The second settlement extends for more than 500 metres along the fen edge. Three groups of contiguous, roughly rectangular enclosures, each with its minor droves, may represent farms and yards. In the largest complex at the east end a rectangular farm enclosure of at least two periods contains a house and other buildings, with which are associated some small rectilinear fields. At some date the area of the enclosure was reduced.[76] In a loose grouping of rectilinear enclosures at West Fen, Willingham (TL 400722), two dwelling sites have been suspected.[77]

The small settlement on a First Terrace gravel 'island' at Upper Delphs, Haddenham (TL 409737), is unusually isolated for the south fenlands. A large regular enclosure contains a smaller enclosure on the south which probably contained the dwelling.

---

[69] Wilson, in *Britannia*, v. 256 and plate xxivb.

[70] Of known settlements 70 per cent are on gravel and more than two thirds are within 1 km. of a waterway. A similar preference for sites near a watercourse but above flood-level has been observed in the valley of the Great Ouse: Green, in *Arch. News Letter*, vol. 5, no. 2, 29–32.

[71] Hallam, in *Roman Fenland*, 58–62.

[72] *Roman Fenland*, 189. On the distinction between regular and irregular fields see above, p. 38.

[73] *Roman Fenland*, 189.

[74] Ibid. 190–1.

[75] Ibid. 192.

[76] Ibid.; 2nd- and 4th-cent. pottery suggests dates for the two phases.

[77] Ibid. 205–6. One site yielded chert masonry, presumably from Cottenham, and 2nd- and 4th-cent. pottery. The more compact group of rectilinear enclosures at Middle Fen, Willingham (TL 402723), yielded chert masonry and 2nd-cent. pottery, and so may have belonged to the same estate. Enclosures around Cut Bridge, Willingham (TL 407729), are similar to those at West Fen.

Finds date mostly to the late 3rd and early 4th centuries, and waterlogging may have ended occupation in the mid 4th.[78] The focus of another settlement in Middle Fen, Willingham (TL 410719), is a large four-sided enclosure approached by a long drove from the south-east and containing the dwellings and farm buildings. Droves led to pasture on the north, and the long drove gave access to strip and rectangular fields on a similar axis. Pottery suggests occupation in the 2nd century and in the late 3rd to early 4th, probably ending in the mid 4th.[79] The same long drove linked the settlement at Middle Fen to the early site at the Sponge north-east, Willingham (TL 419715), whose main feature is a nearly rectangular double-ditched enclosure with some nearly rectangular enclosures on the south associated with a long drove to the west.[80] Immediately south-west lies the later site at the Sponge south-east (TL 418714), where the earliest pottery dates to the 2nd century A.D. A long drove leads north-west, on a line roughly parallel to that connecting Middle Fen with the Sponge north-east, and joins some smaller droves or lanes from different directions. Near the junction are two circular features which have been interpreted as a mill and threshing floor. A rectangular enclosure is associated with short lanes on the east. Traces of fields are also visible on the north. To the south-east are some ill defined settlements around the Stacks, Willingham.[81]

The settlement at Meadow Drove, Willingham (TL 433708), begins in the early 2nd century and may continue into the early 4th. It comprises complete and incomplete rectilinear enclosures representing dwellings, yards, and fields. A single ditch runs east from the settlement to a gravel island, whence a ditch runs almost due south. South-west of the angle and aligned to it is the rectangular enclosure at the Hempsals, Willingham (TL 436706). It has open access on the south-west, along the south side of what was probably the focal enclosure, into a long rectangular area on the east where animals may have been penned overnight.[82] Of two adjacent settlements located on the Ampthill Clay, in contrast to the more usual position on the gravel edge, that at Glebe Farm south-west, Willingham (TL 435714), is not easily defined but includes small enclosures and rectilinear fields linked to an east-west drove and has produced 2nd- and 4th-century pottery and corallian limestone from Upware indicating masonry construction. A drove approaches from the south and another leads northwards to wetter alluvial areas. Similar pottery has been found on the other site at Glebe Farm south-east, Willingham (TL 438713), which is a nucleated group of enclosures separated by lanes which lead north, west, and south.[83] A similar site at Smithey Fen central, Cottenham (TL 446713), lies on the edge of the Ampthill Clay which defines the alluvium. It consists of roughly rectangular enclosures probably representing dwellings, farmyards, and paddocks. The pottery belongs mainly to the 2nd century with a few pieces of the late 3rd and 4th centuries. In the late period the focus of the settlement may have shifted to the south (TL 449711).[84] The remains of Oxholme Drove, Cottenham (TL 449704), further south on a gravel spur, are in a rectilinear pattern less densely packed than in the previous settlement. A remarkable small site at Oxholme Drove (TL 451702) has a rectangular enclosure at the end of a drove from the Ampthill Clay, while another leads from the east away from the gravel edge towards the enclosure. South-east of the main enclosure lie a smaller rectangular and an L-shaped

[78] *Roman Fenland*, 206.
[79] Ibid. 207.
[80] Ibid. 207–8. Surface finds of pottery indicate an Iron Age origin for the double-ditched enclosure.
[81] Ibid. 207.
[82] Ibid. 209. Pottery from the Hempsals site is of the 2nd and 3rd cents.

[83] Ibid. 210–11. A ditch bounding the two settlements on the N. and running from Pound Ground to Smithey Fen may have drained the area of pasture which it defined.
[84] Ibid. 211–12. Sinuous lengths of ditch, perhaps defining fields, linked the settlement to gravel lands on the E.

enclosure, indicating perhaps a small farm where cattle were stalled in the main enclosure after being driven from pasture.[85]

Perhaps the largest settlement on the southern edge of the fenlands was at Bullock's
Haste, Cottenham (TL 465704), extending along both sides (mainly the west) of the
Car Dyke (Old Tillage). Rectilinear enclosures adjoin a meandering lane or drove from
which several subsidiary ways diverge. On both sides of the lane in a continuous block
some enclosures contain closely spaced parallel ditches whose function is not clear,
while others contained dwellings with yards and gardens. South of the main lane
regular fields are bounded by a parallel subsidiary lane, and similar fields lie beyond
the north end of the main drove. Finds that include a bust of Commodus (180–92)
indicate that this was no ordinary agricultural settlement and may have been a commercial and religious centre for the area. Pottery of all periods has been discovered and
some buildings were of stone.[86]

Occupation of the 2nd and 4th centuries is recorded at Grange Farm, Stretham (TL
499723), which lies on the Kimmeridge Clay and consists of rectilinear fields within
long boundary ditches, while other apparent field systems were arranged in similar
fashion further north-east towards the edge of the Kimmeridge Clay outcrop at New
Road, Stretham (TL 512733), where pottery of the 2nd and 3rd centuries has been
found. Along with the settlement at Starlock Hay Fen (TL 519738), which also lies on
the Kimmeridge clay, it may have belonged to an estate centred on the villa at Tiled
House Farm, Stretham (TL 523732), the only villa so far identified in the area. The
principal buildings were set on the Lower Greensand, noted for its dryness. Occupation began in the earlier 2nd century and continued into the 5th, with some suggestion
of a recession in the 3rd. In the 4th century there was a familiar arrangement of rooms
and outbuildings around a court, with the original nucleus of the residence placed on
one side.[87]

Across the river Cam was a substantial settlement at Barway, Soham (TL 543752),
part of which at New Fordey Farm comprises enclosures and fields aligned and connected with a T-junction of two droves, whence has come pottery from the late 1st
century to the 4th. The rest of the settlement lies north of a drove which joins a lane
connecting it with the nucleus. More than one phase of settlement is indicated by the
remains. The small riverside site at Upware, Wicken (TL 538701), appears to be of
the same type.[88]

A group of settlements lies on the gravels south of Bullock's Haste. That at Mitchell
Hill, Cottenham (TL 477700), has very small rectangular and nearly square enclosures
adjoining a drove and disposed as around a yard. The site at Top Moor, Cottenham
(TL 483689), differs from its neighbours on the south and has an outer, roughly
rectangular ditched enclosure, containing an irregular enclosure with a wide entrance
at its south corner, and in the south-west are three circular structures of uncertain
purpose, possibly religious.[89] To the south a large area was divided by a framework of
three large droves, two running roughly east-west 480 to 520 metres apart and the
third at right angles. The rectangle thus formed enclosed some large rectilinear fields
in a regular alignment and at the centre a trapezoidal enclosure (TL 480683); 2nd-
century pottery comes from a rectangular enclosure attached to the north ditch of

[85] Ibid. 211–12. Both sites yielded 2nd- and 4th-cent.
pottery.
[86] See Plate VA. Clark, in *Antiq. Jnl.* xxix. 145–63; cf.
Roman Fenland, 212–14; for the bust and other finds see
below, pp. 80–1.
[87] *Roman Fenland*, 215, 226–7. A coin-hoard near the

site (TL 52327298) attests occupation into the 3rd decade
of the 5th cent.: J. W. E. Pearce, in *Proc. C.A.S.* xxxix
(1940), 85–92.
[88] *Roman Fenland*, 227–8.
[89] Ibid. 204. The pottery shows occupation from the mid
2nd cent. to the 5th.

the southern drove (TL 481681). A settlement to the east, with limiting ditches south of the drove and a rectangular enclosure bounded on three sides by lanes and tracks attached at the south end of the west drove to its west side, existed at Green End, Cottenham (TL 474682), and has produced native pottery and wares of the late 1st and 2nd century. A long rectangular block of enclosures was attached at the centre to the north ditch of the northern drove, with its main axis at a right angle to it, from which has come 2nd- and early-3rd-century pottery. Another settlement at Cottenham, Top Moor (TL 481686), exhibits more than one phase of settlement but seems to show signs of the large-scale planning that might be expected on a single estate containing several farms spaced regularly and connected by lanes.[90]

Of two settlements to the north-east, Denny Lodge, Waterbeach (TL 499692), consists of large enclosures linked to some connecting and intersecting droves. There is also a field divided into strips by parallel ditches similar to enclosures at Bullock's Haste. Pottery from the site extends from the early 2nd century to possibly the early 4th. Linked to the settlement was one at Chittering, Waterbeach (TL 503694), where two groups of enclosures lie either side of a wide lane: the southern group is connected by a ditch to the Denny Lodge settlement and the northern contains a circular structure. The 'grid-iron' ditches of the site have been suggested as designed to hold wooden traps which could be lowered in water.[91]

A belt of settlements extended along both banks of the Cam as far as Cambridge. Settlements on the gravels around the south edge of the fenlands are a continuation of those in the upland valleys further south, the distinction between the two areas being perhaps in density rather than in character. At First Public Drain, Histon (TL 434627), where a villa may have existed, there are signs of rectilinear enclosures. Some villas west of the Cam along the fenland skirt may match those along the chalk edge. At the Gravel Pits, Milton (TL 482623), two kilns attest local pottery production in the late 1st century and early 2nd. At Rampton Road, Longstanton (TL 402672), what appears to be an irregular field system of the Wyboston type was replaced later by rectilinear fields and straight droves of the St. Ives type.[92]

Roman settlements in the northern fenlands show some marked differences from those in the south and are more varied. Among a large concentration of Roman settlement north and east of March some examples from Wimblington may be selected for comment. The pre-Roman site at Stonea Camp (TL 448931) has produced samian pottery of the Claudian–Neronian period (TL 448931). There are rectilinear enclosures, possibly with associated fields, in March, near Stonea Grange (TL 448945), which has produced mortared stone and at least one well-appointed building.[93] Near the Golden Lion Inn at Stonea, in Wimblington (TL 460934), a hut within an enclosure was occupied from the early 2nd century to the early 3rd. At Stonebridge Farm, Stonea (TL 462941), the settlement consists of rectangular enclosures, while a small isolated enclosure is known close to an old watercourse at Wateringhill Farm, Manea (TL 476936).[94]

North-east of some irregular enclosures and fields, along with numerous pits, at Earl's Fen, March (TL 455949), is the substantial settlement of Earl's Fen, north

---

[90] *Roman Fenland*, 202–3.
[91] Ibid. 205, 224–5. Excavation showed a very shallow ditch and circular and rectangular settings of stakeholes.
[92] Ibid. 198–9, 201.
[93] Ibid. 218–19. Native stonework is unknown in the area. A mosaic at Stonea Grange, Wimblington (TL 449938), indicates a substantial building; the site yielded a

3rd-cent. coin hoard. Another substantial building was at Hardings Drain, Wimblington (TL 453934).
[94] *Roman Fenland*, 219–20. Debris from Stonebridge Farm included pottery, animal bones, querns, a spindle-whorl, and briquetage. For the Golden Lion site see T. W. J. Potter, in *Proc. C.A.S.* lxvi (1977), 37–54.

(TL 458953), where two blocks of irregular and roughly rectangular enclosures were attached to the north-west and south-east corners of a larger enclosure, with an entrance on the south approached by a curving drove. Irregular strips on the north probably represent fields. The settlement appears to have been a loose agglomeration rather than a closely related set of enclosures. Linked to the Earl's Fen settlement by a ditch is that at Bedlam Farm, March (TL 460956), a similar loose grouping of rectangular enclosures.[95]

The settlement at Russell's Farm, Upwell (TL 477957), formed by a cluster of enclosures by an old watercourse, has produced daub, bricks, pottery, and fire-bars perhaps from corn-drying ovens.[96] Beyond a small group of irregular enclosures at the Water Wheel, Upwell (TL 475963), the settlement at Well Fen Farm (TL 470979) is aligned on the Rodham Farm Canal and the Fen Causeway which lie on the north. The focus was rectangular and some less regular enclosures extend along the line of the canal; some of them were certainly dwelling-sites with fields and paddocks attached on the south, which in the extreme south have the form of parallel strips 240 by 67·5 metres. The fields and settlement at the Hill, Christchurch in Upwell (TL 494968), further east along the causeway, are a truly nucleated close group with in some places a grid plan of small enclosures and droves, linked by a single long drove to a block of regular rectilinear fields on the west adapted to the natural waterways. The drove running west from the nucleus turns north to form the west limit of the fields and meets the Fen Causeway at a right angle. Evidently the construction of the fields was later than or closely linked with that of the causeway. A site north of the causeway at West's Farm, Upwell (TL 498979), consists of roughly rectangular enclosures, including some houses and yards, and rectilinear fields to the west. Pottery of the 2nd and 3rd centuries has been found there. Further north a small settlement by the Sixteen Foot Drain, Upwell (TL 492988), consists of a few enclosures around the junction of some short droves. A group of fields and enclosures is arranged irregularly and linked with an extinct stream at Euximoor Fen, Upwell (TL 466989), beyond which on the west are some strip fields c. 150 by 30·5 metres. On the north bank further along the same stream the small settlement at Holbourn Farm, March (TL 457998), comprises a compact group of small enclosures with perhaps some ditched fields north of the stream. On the south are some strip fields c. 185 by 15·5 metres. South of that group of settlements the Rodham Farm settlement (TL 459982) has regular enclosures and ditches, in which a hut was discovered beneath 30 cm. of silt on the levée of the canal.[97]

Some sites further south may be noted. There is an extensive system of irregularly disposed fields with associated ring ditches at Cawthorne's Farm, Chatteris (TL 396822). Occupation at Primrose Hill, Doddington (TL 384896), is recorded by pottery and a hearth in a settlement that was covered by peat as conditions became wetter in the post-Roman, perhaps in the late Roman, period. Droves and enclosures are known at Block Fen, Chatteris (TL 427837), and Langwood Hill, Chatteris (TL 417853), in the latter associated with a rectangular stone building. Irregular enclosures at Honey Hill, Chatteris (TL 433890), are associated with a field system, while a hearth, together with tile and fired clay, was excavated at Honey Bridge, Wimblington (TL 435893). At Thirties Farm, March (TL 449956), a western outlier of the group of settlements at Earl's Fen and Bedlam Farm, the plan remains unintelligible but includes ring ditches

[95] *Roman Fenland*, 219, 222.
[96] Ibid. 222–3. Possible inhumation burials are known. Two large groups of long parallel strips, perhaps associated with the site if not post-Roman, are linked by a dog-legged ditch which defined the E. group on the N. and the W. group on the E. In the latter the strips are up to 600 by 38 metres.
[97] *Roman Fenland*, 222–3.

and areas defined by straight stretches of ditch, with a watercourse close by to the north.[98]

An unbroken landscape of Roman settlement extended across a large area north-east of March, with a major settlement at Flaggrass, March (TL 434985), whose focus lay in the north-west angle formed by the Fen Causeway and the Flaggrass waterway. Lying on the edge of a gravel island the enclosures of the settlement are aligned on the watercourse, while the soakaway ditch provides a boundary on the west. Pottery from all parts of the site, including the line of the waterway, suggests that the channel went out of use during the life of the Roman settlement. The arrangement consists of roughly rectangular strips at about right angles to the watercourse; some strips are subdivided, and some lie south of the Fen Causeway. Regular fields lie east of the waterway and a few may exist south of the causeway. Pottery dates from the late 1st century to the 4th, and a great variety of finds attests iron-working and salt-production, indicating that the settlement was an industrial as well as an agricultural centre.[99] A similar settlement with smaller enclosures and rectilinear fields lay north of Flaggrass at Twenty Foot River, March (TL 434992), while that at Creek Road, March (TL 440987), to the east is less regular with small rectangular enclosures around the junction of four droves; one drove leads to the Fen Causeway and the others to fields north and east, which being defined by watercourses are less regularly planned. The east drove at Creek Road led to a more regular settlement of rectangular enclosures at Frank's Farm, March (TL 445989), near the T-junction of three droves, where a trapezoid enclosure on the north is divided internally by ditches into thin strips, in the fashion already observed at Bullock's Haste. Some form of stone platform and a gravel track may have existed at Middle Level Yard, March (TL 421968). Due west of Flaggrass the settlement at Estover Cottage, March (TL 422984), close to the likely line of the Fen Causeway, consists of roughly rectangular enclosures disposed north of a drove, and further west is an isolated double-ditched enclosure at Westry Farm, March (TL 401988).[1]

Excavation of the 15-ha. settlement at Grandford, March (TL 393996), on the line of the Fen Causeway, with a fairly regular layout of enclosures separated by lanes, has shown occupation continuing to the end of the 4th century. Occupation of the central part began as early as c. A.D. 65–70 when ditches were dug to prevent waterlogging, which appears to have recurred in the 3rd century. Besides some substantial buildings finds suggest a local workshop producing bone implements.[2] At Longhill Farm, March (TL 407994), some rectilinear fields and smaller enclosures are linked with a drove leading to the West Water on the north, where other enclosures are known at Norwood House, March (TL 414999). Norwood (TL 418995), where rectilinear enclosures lie on both sides of a stream, yielded pottery from the late 1st century to the 4th, loom-weights, a quern, a premature infant burial beneath a hut floor, and signs of salt-production.[3] The area of close but irregular enclosures at Stag's Holt south, March (TF 438001), has produced much pottery and saltern refuse, which may have come from Stag's Holt east (TF 434004) where dispersed enclosures were attached to part of a drove connected with fields in the north and west. To the north-west the settlement at Rutlands south, Elm (TF 431009), lies within the meander of a watercourse with unplanned and irregular enclosures but with droves leading to fields and water-meadows. North of the stream huts and rubbish pits have been examined at Rutlands west (TF

---

[98] *Roman Fenland*, 195, 215–16, 222. Some features may not be of Roman date.

[99] See Plate VB. *Roman Fenland*, 221–2. Finds include 2nd- and late-3rd-cent. coin hoards, inhumation burials, personal ornaments, glass, an inscribed stone since lost, and loom-weights.   [1] *Roman Fenland*, 220–2.

[2] Ibid. 197. A 3rd-cent. building had a tile roof and glazed windows.   [3] Ibid. 220.

428015). On the east a close-knit group of small enclosures at Coldham Field, Elm (TF 433015), lies in the angle at the junction of two droves, and is connected with the stream on the south and fields on the east attached to a long drove which joins an even longer one from the Coldham Hall settlement, described below.[4]

To the south-east an extensive belt of settlement with small irregular enclosures at White House Farm east, Elm (TF 445006), exists within the curve of a watercourse levée, whence has come late-3rd- and early-4th-century pottery. At White House Farm north (TF 441010) there is an unusual arrangement of an irregular double-ditched enclosure with a precisely rectangular enclosure on the south divided equally. North of the watercourse the settlement at Creekgall Fen, Elm (TF 450012), consists of close-knit small enclosures with associated droves, including one leading to Coldham Bank south, Elm. There pottery and structures have been found, perhaps corn-drying ovens, and what has been interpreted as 'a wagon with a netted load of barley'. Other settlements include White Mill Drain, Upwell (TF 456011), where leather sandals have been found, and still further east a small settlement with strip fields at Riverside Farm, Upwell (TF 461006), and Low Corner Farm, Upwell (TF 469008), where huts have been discovered.[5]

The settlement made up of rectangular enclosures at Coldham Bank south, Elm (TF 447017), separates the Creekgall Fen site from the large settlement at Coldham Hall, Elm (TF 442025), where among many finds pottery indicates occupation from the early 2nd century to the late 4th. Huts with clay floors lie within circular ditches. Small enclosures have been recognized at the junction of several droves and some larger fields overlain by strips, where much pottery has been found. At Coldham Bank north, Elm (TF 448023), the sweep of the bank has determined an irregular arrangement of dwellings, droves, and fields, although more regular fields on the north are linked by a drove. A pottery kiln has been reported there, and a 3rd-century coin hoard (TF 452022). A drove links the settlement with the round ditch of a settlement at Coldham Clamp, Elm (TF 448027), where occupation extends from c. A.D. 70 or slightly later to c. 200. There is an example of an isolated single rectilinear settlement at Coldham Station, Elm (TF 433028), divided into two parts, with a short spur of ditch from the south-west corner.[6]

West of Waldersea Hall, Elm (TF 448035), is an irregular arrangement of enclosures and on the east a close-knit group of small rectangular enclosures including hut circles (TF 451034). At Laddus Farm, Elm (TF 473017), where there is a loose grouping of roughly rectangular enclosures either side of a lane, huts have been discovered and six inhumation burials excavated. A more regular arrangement of fields, with associated enclosures and long strips on two alignments at right angles, is at Hundred Acre Farm, Elm (TF 475022), where huts and inhumation burials have also been found. Huts are known at other settlements in the vicinity, Forties Farm, Elm (TF 472028), Sluice Farm, Upwell (TF 482014), and Fluke Cottage Farm, Upwell (TF 485023). Another extensive belt of settlement exists at Needham Hall Field, Elm (TF 488042), where appears a pattern of linked clusters of small irregular enclosures with associated watercourses and fields. Enclosures are larger and more loosely arranged in the north, where the fields lie. Huts have been discovered on the site, where occupation began in the early 2nd century. To the east lies an area of poorly defined enclosures and fields (TF 496043) and east again, just within the county, is a small group of enclosures near a watercourse at Gilbert Cottage, Outwell (TF 502037).[7]

[4] Ibid. 317–18.
[6] Ibid. 318–20. Finds at Coldham Hall include saltern
[5] Ibid. 319–21.   debris, beads, pewter, and an inhumation with a bronze bracelet.
[7] Ibid. 321–2, 327.

Further west some enclosures at Percival Farm, Elm (TF 433036), were linked closely with a stream, with which the major settlement further north at Waldersea, Elm (TF 432049), is also linked, where the enclosure focus is somewhat irregular on the levée of the watercourse. On the north-east strips 200 by 20 metres may represent remains of Roman ploughing, since this part of the fens was not reclaimed until Tudor times. A close-knit group of small regular enclosures at Hogg's Farm, Wisbech St. Peter (TF 418050), lies on the western branch of the same stream. Further north-west a palimpsest of earthworks at Inlay's Farm, Wisbech St. Mary (TF 408057), belongs to different periods: some may be Roman.[8]

Among several settlements identified in the parishes of Wisbech St. Mary and Wisbech St. Peter a rectilinear field pattern, with no obvious focus, is found at Red-moor Field (TF 438063), while huts have been found at Crooked Bank (TF 450063) and Nymandole Farm (TF 431087). Loose arrangements of fields and enclosures are known at Calves' Field (TF 397055), Murrow Field (TF 385065), and smaller and more compact at Old South Eau Bank (TF 379057). Obviously nucleated clusters of irregular enclosures are known at Murrow station (TF 362063), around an old river course and with an associated drove, and on the north at North Level Drain, Parson Drove (TF 360067). A more regular arrangement is known at South Inham Field, Parson Drove (TF 375077), where circular ditches are succeeded by rectangular structures set within well-ordered ditched enclosures. The traces of a palimpsest of irregularly disposed rectangular and sub-rectangular enclosures at College Lots Farm, Parson Drove (TF 367078), are less obvious than those of a compact group of enclosures associated with fields and watercourses at Mill Drain, Parson Drove (TF 352068). Further north is a group of small enclosures, not regularly planned but linked to a major drove system, at Johnson's Drove (TF 353077), which leads towards other settlements on the west and a large complex to the north. A system of partly rectilinear fields was associated with this settlement.[9]

The major group of settlements to the north consists of sites linked by a system of roughly rectilinear droves, giving a superficial impression of an integrated pattern. Sites include enclosures and connecting droves at Bleak House, Parson Drove (TF 359087), while on the county boundary with Lincolnshire the core of Coles Bridge, Sutton St. Edmund (TF 354092), is a junction of several droves around which are grouped some very small enclosures.[10] A large group of enclosures of various sizes is found to the north-east at Throckenholt, Sutton St. Edmund (TF 358094). The south-west boundary is formed by a long ditch which continues south-eastwards to form a similar definition for Clough's Cross, Parson Drove (TF 367090), where some of a group of regular enclosures contain circles north of a bifurcating drove. A similar concentration of settlement is found to the west and south-west. On the south-east fringe a small group of rectangular enclosures is linked by a drove to Parson Drove Fen (TF 346076), which is defined on the south-west by a long drove which continues north-westwards to define boundaries of settlements in the Lincolnshire fens. Parson Drove Fen is linked to the settlement at the Grange, Parson Drove (TF 343075), where regular enclosures lie alongside the branches of a T-shaped drove junction. A larger site at Inkerson Fen, Parson Drove (TF 343069), includes several linked clusters of rectangular enclosures with an associated drove near a waterway. A similar but more closely grouped settlement occurs at Common Road, Parson Drove (TF 340077). Several sites are aligned on and attached to the boundary drove, including the regular rectangular enclosures in Thorney at Inkerson Grange (TF 335068).[11]

---

[8] *Roman Fenland*, 318, 322.   [9] Ibid. 297–8, 323.   [10] See Plate VIB.   [11] *Roman Fenland*, 296–7.

Analysis of Roman settlements in the Lincolnshire fens, closely comparable to those of Cambridgeshire, has suggested four main types of settlement distinguished by layout. First is the small irregular settlements which developed within the limits of meandering streams, where numerous small ditches were dug for drainage and where industrial debris is often found. That type is believed to have developed before the end of the 1st century. The second type consists of a loose association of small farms spaced at intervals of up to 400 metres. Third come the large irregular groups which developed in the 2nd century and coalesced into extensive belts of continuous settlement. The very different fourth type consists of regularly planned farms, often associated with rectilinear layouts, which represent fresh foundations of the second quarter of the 2nd century. Around the mid 2nd century there developed groups of settlements which combined features of the earlier irregular types with those of later rectilinear types. At the same time a more open type evolved, less dispersed than the loose arrangements of some early-2nd-century settlements, while the more compact layouts of the 2nd century are well represented in Cambridgeshire. Groups of enclosures appear in close-knit clusters with both regular and irregular layouts. In some regular settlements there is subgrouping of enclosures, indicating perhaps the juxtaposition of separate economic units. In some cases the more compact groups are so irregularly arranged that it is almost impossible to identify a focus. The newer compact arrangements developed during the 3rd century, when a notable feature was a tightness of the clustering. Settlement that was extensive but compact and densely occupied was the main type to survive through to the end of the Roman period. General conclusions on the Lincolnshire evidence suggested 'a total picture of farms scattered but not isolated, falling mainly into small groups with some larger agglomerations'. Furthermore it is such 'patterns of loose groupings from which some nucleations emerge'.[12]

The dimensions of most settlements can usually be roughly determined by surface remains. Few sites less than 15 metres long are recorded, only 15 per cent in the 1st century and less than 10 in later periods. Larger sites between 15 and 45 metres form 53 per cent of the total in the late 1st century, 54 in the 2nd and 3rd, and 61 in the 4th. The rest fall into two groups, one of about 75 by 45 metres, the other of between 90 by 70 and 125 by 90 metres. A refuse spread of 30 by 25 metres was most common with the class of sites measuring 15 to 30 metres in length, which may indicate that the dimensions of the average toft were slightly less. The larger categories may represent the refuse scattered over a whole farm complex or a whole settlement within which individual units cannot be readily identified. It emerged clearly that in Lincolnshire settlements were not distributed altogether at random but were to a certain degree concentrated.[13]

There remains the difficult problem of status, where such notions as 'farm', 'hamlet', and 'village' may be anachronistic. The study of Lincolnshire has demonstrated that most nuclei in Roman settlement could be assigned the status of 'multiple unit', and it was possible to demonstrate the contemporaneity of several sites within the same settlement. There seems little doubt that all four classes of settlement are to be found also in the Cambridgeshire fens: the 'single farm' consisting of a settlement with a single site, the 'small hamlet' comprising a settlement with two or three sites, the 'large hamlet' with four to six sites, and last the 'small village' with seven or more sites. As in Lincolnshire there was in the Cambridgeshire fenlands a progression from loosely scattered settlements towards more concentrated zones of occupation.

[12] Hallam, in *Roman Fenland*, 22–88, esp. 58–62, analyses Lincs. settlements.
[13] Ibid. 49–51.

Distribution was more scattered on the inland fenlands and more concentrated nearer the sea.[14]

The status of the fenlands within the Roman province remains unknown, although the possibility has long been entertained that they formed an imperial estate, whose western boundary may have been defined by a fragmentary inscription from Sawtry (Hunts.) near Ermine Street reading PVBLIC[. . .].[15] Moreover it is reasonable to argue that the extensive drainage works and long droves required considerable engineering skill and planning by public surveyors (*mensores*), while the expense of such a co-ordinated undertaking was too great for a private estate. There is, however, little sign of over-all regular planning, and local schemes effected by individual settlements suggest substantial continuity of a local population. The general absence of villas and high-quality imports suggests a countryside of smallholders perhaps holding leases directly from an imperial agency, rather than the more widespread arrangement of tenants (*coloni*) leasing farms from the absentee proprietors of large private estates. On the analogy of other provinces the area was administered by an imperial land agent (*procurator saltus*), perhaps more than one if the Fen Causeway divided the fenlands between the Severan provinces of Upper and Lower Britain. Local agents (*conductores*) managed the rent due from the tenants whose leases ran often for the five years of the Roman *census*, with concessionary rates for those who took on difficult or perhaps newly reclaimed land. The salt-workings of the north fenlands are likely to have been controlled by the imperial agents and officials. In almost all respects, financially and juridically, the procuratorial administration was capable of fulfilling the role of city, an institution whose absence from the fenlands is perhaps the strongest pointer to some special status for the area.[16]

The status of the fenland skirt is less easily defined. The pattern of settlement includes the additional element of Roman villas, which in the east seem closely related to the lodes. The lodes are likely to have been planned by Roman engineers. Perhaps the villas were residences of local imperial officials (*conductores*), and it is difficult to avoid the conclusion that the skirtlands exhibit regular layouts resulting from officially instigated schemes.[17]

Finally what may have been a distinctive feature of the areas bordering the fenlands, and perhaps other parts of south Cambridgeshire, is the association between villa and 'village', which has been more clearly demonstrated at places outside the county.[18] The relationship may have been comparable with that between manor and village in medieval times, although there is no reason to suggest that for most of the Roman period the population of the 'villages' was unfree. Rents were probably paid in kind, and the generally low level of coinage in the country-side might suggest that few received money wages. It has been suggested that in the late Roman period tenants on the imperial property in the siltlands were *vicani*, tied to a particular village or district, while those in the south were tenants (*coloni*) tied to the estates of the landowners by the legal obligations defined under Constantine I in the early 4th century.[19] During the earlier Roman period the nature of land-holding and ownership might have changed markedly, and such changes may underlie the variations in forms and pattern of settlement that have been described above.

[14] Hallam, *Roman Fen'and*, 51–3.

[15] Garrood, in *Antiq. Jnl.* xx (1940), 504–5 and plate xcii; *J.R.S.* xxx (1940), 186 no. 14; cf. Hallam, in *Roman Fenland*, 70; for the inscription, Collingwood and Wright, *Roman Inscr. of Britain*, i, no. 230.

[16] The problems of the status of the fenlands are examined by Salway, in *Roman Fenland*, 10–12, whose conclusions are summarized here.

[17] Ibid. 12. A site at Mildenhall (Suff.) (TL 686794) yielded an amphora handle from property confiscated by Septimius Severus after the defeat of Clodius Albinus at Lugdunum, A.D. 197: Hartley, in *Antiq. Jnl.* xxxviii (1958), 91–2.

[18] Salway, in *Roman Fenland*, 12.

[19] Ibid. 17.

PLATE I

ERMINE STREET, looking north-north-west from Caxton (TL 305579), showing the change of alignment north of Caxton. [p. 17]

PLATE II

B. The Fen Causeway, looking east from east of March (TL 437983). [pp. 22–3]

A. Reach Village, from the south-east (TL 560657), showing the Devil's Ditch and Reach Lode. [pp. 6, 11]

PLATE III

A. THE VILLA AT GUILDEN MORDEN from north-north-east (TL 277405). [p. 46]

B. THE CEMETERY AT LITLINGTON from the north (TL 314420). [p. 86]

PLATE IV

B. The Villa at Reach from the north (TL 572652). [p. 45]

A. Possible Villa at Allington Hill, Bottisham, from the north-west (TL 578588). [p. 46]

PLATE V

A. BULLOCK'S HASTE, COTTENHAM, from the north (TL 465704), showing the settlement extending along the Car Dyke. [p. 49]

B. THE SETTLEMENT AT FLAGGRASS, MARCH, from the south-east (TL 434984), showing the Fen Causeway running west crossed by the Flaggrass waterway running north, with the focus of settlement in the north-west angle of the junction. [p. 52]

PLATE VI

A. THE AREA BETWEEN ARBURY ROAD AND KINGS HEDGES, seen from the south-east (TL 454612) with Akeman Street running diagonally from the lower left-hand corner and crossing the First Public Drain short of the upper right-hand corner. [pp. 19, 44]

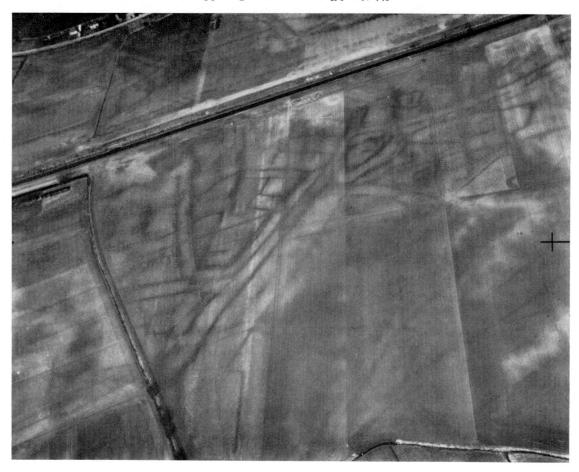

B. SETTLEMENT NEAR COLES BRIDGE, from the south (TF 355090). New South Eau, across the upper part of the picture, is the boundary between Parson Drove (Cambs.) and Sutton St. Edmund (Lincs.). [p. 54]

PLATE VII

A. GLASS FLASK AND JUG from Hauxton Mill ($\frac{1}{3}$).
[p. 84]

B. SARDONYX INTAGLIO DEPICTING EROS from Shepreth ($\frac{11}{4}$). [p. 66]

C. GLASS FLAGON from Barnwell ($\frac{1}{3}$). [p. 84n]

D. BRONZE HEAD of male Celtic Deity from Girton ($\frac{1}{1}$).
[p. 82]

PLATE VIII

A. Fragment of a column from Carter's Well, Grant-chester ($\frac{1}{3}$)

C. Lion's Head from Girton ($\frac{1}{5}$)

D. Head in cornice from Arbury Road ($\frac{1}{2}$)

Part of male torso, seen from the back, wearing belt and probably a tunic. From the Roman & Anglo-Saxon cemetery. Girton College.

B. Torso from Girton ($\frac{1}{4}$)

E. Rosette in Cornice from Arbury Road ($\frac{2}{7}$)

SCULPTURED STONE [pp. 67–8]

PLATE IX

A, B. Figured Pot from Horningsea ($\frac{2}{5}$). [p. 73]

C. Waster from Jesus Lane, Cambridge ($\frac{2}{3}$). [pp. 73–4]

D. Pottery Vessel with neck-mask from Cambridge ($\frac{4}{5}$). [p. 86n]

POTTERY

PLATE X

A. Bowls From Burwell $(\frac{3}{20})$

B. Imported Jugs From Hauxton $(\frac{2}{7})$

BRONZE [pp. 78–9]

PLATE XI

A. Bronze Statuettes of Diana (from Bassingbourn), Mercury (Manea Fen), Hercules (Sutton), Venus (Ely), and a genius walking (Ely) (½). [pp. 81–2]

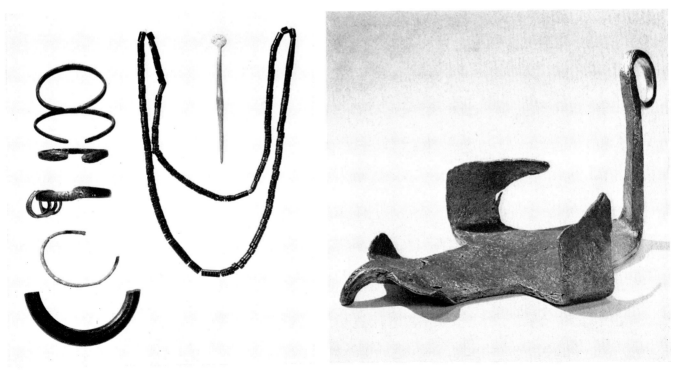

B. Necklace, Bone Pin, and Bracelets from an inhumation at Linton (⅖). [pp. 89–90]

C. Iron Hippo-sandal from Arrington Bridge (½). [p. 78]

PLATE XII

C. Handle of Bronze Skillet from near Prickwillow ($\frac{5}{6}$). [p. 78]

A, B. Pewter Tazza with Christian symbols, possibly from Sutton; top and side views ($\frac{2}{7}$). [pp. 83, 86]

PLATE XIII

A. Pewter Jugs from Roll's Lode, Isleham Fen, and Burwell ($\frac{2}{9}$). [p. 83]

B. Grave Goods from the Litlington cemetery ($\frac{3}{8}$). [pp. 86–7]

PLATE XIV

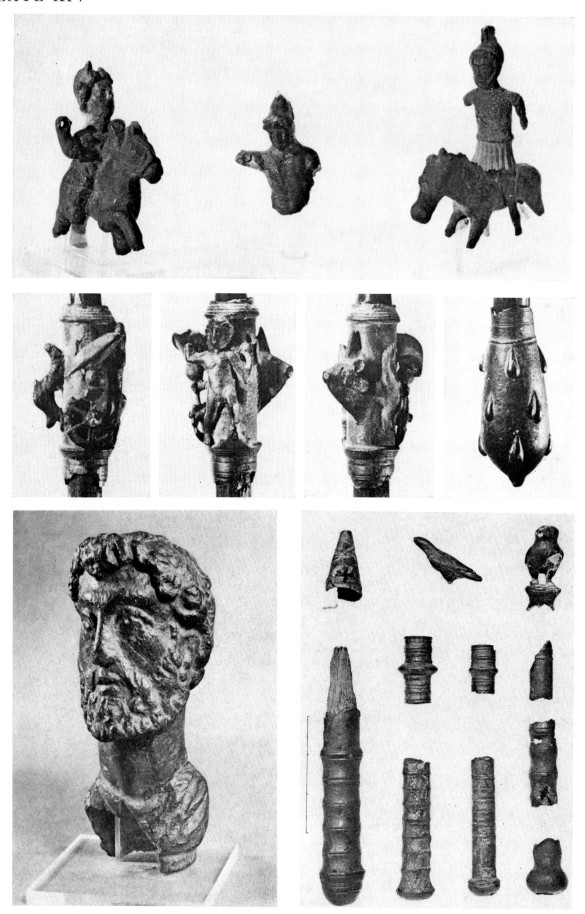

A. From Arbury Road (⅕)

B. From Girton (²⁄₇)

CREMATION GROUPS [p. 87]

PLATE XVI

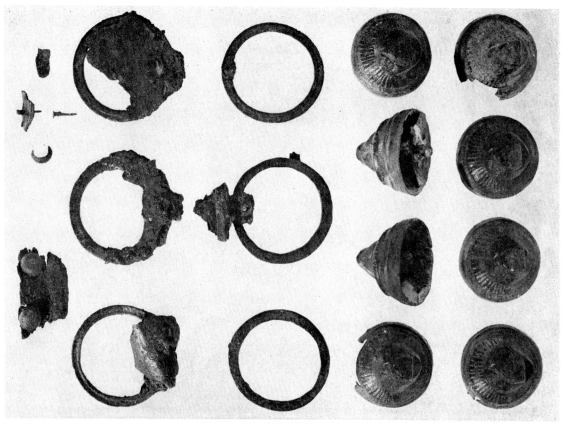

C. Bronze Bosses from a Girton cremation group ($\frac{4}{7}$). [p. 87]

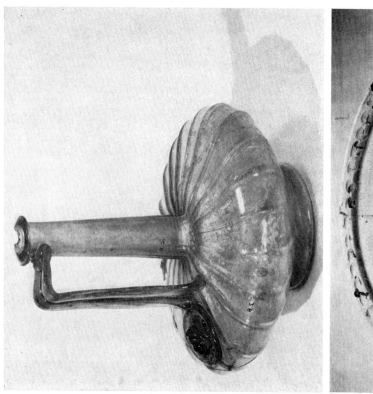

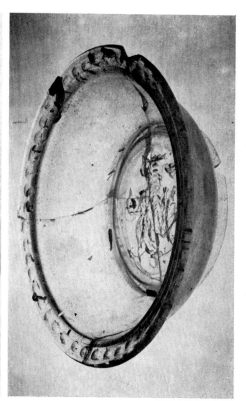

A. Glass Jug from Litlington ($\frac{4}{7}$). [p. 84]

B. The Glass 'Duck Bowl' from Girton ($\frac{9}{20}$). [pp. 84, 87]

South Cambridgeshire

Both crop-marks observed on aerial photographs and surface finds indicate extensive Roman settlement on the valley gravels and, in a smaller way, on the chalklands. What follows is only a selection of the sites recorded, chosen to indicate the variety of settlement known to have existed away from the fenlands. On the gravel terraces north of Cambridge between the true fenlands and the valley lands of the south there was an extensive settlement associated with the kilns at Horningsea (TL 496634).[20] Further south is a settlement of *c.* 2 ha. (TL 488619) where the principal element appears to be a single enclosure, within three ditches which form an enclosure open to the river Cam on the north-west. The area between the central and outer enclosure measures more than 30 metres across. A drove from the river leads to a paddock within the outer enclosure, which might suggest an arrangement similar to the Wyboston type found in the fenlands. The functions of other subdivisions, and other enclosures attached to the outer enclosure, remain obscure, although some may have contained farm buildings while others were perhaps fields. The over-all impression is of a single farm based on cattle and arable in the manner of fenland sites, although the general layout seems to contain a number of Roman features.[21] Another settlement further south-east (TL 491611) occupied a similar area with associated fields and other enclosures. Although the general layout is roughly rectangular many of the ditch-lines are curved.[22]

Surface finds at Grange Farm, Lode (TL 54006325), show a Roman settlement where four rectangular buildings are revealed by areas of white soil *c.* 9 by 4·5 metres. Pottery indicates an occupation from the 2nd century to the 4th, and other finds include limestone, roof- and box-tiles, window glass, and grass-marked baked clay.[23] The principal element of the regular settlement at Fen Ditton (TL 50356008) is a rectangular enclosure 155 by 60 metres; the southern half is subdivided into a set of small enclosures which presumably contained buildings, since the southern third of the enclosure appears to be marked off from the remainder by a fence and ditch, and was perhaps the residential area. Long straight ditches lead from both south corners, which may be linked with other ditches further south. The enclosures may have been pasture rather than arable fields.[24]

An example of a settlement on chalkland is at War Ditches, Cherry Hinton (TL 484556), where some postholes have been interpreted as three rectangular buildings of two periods, one Antonine, the second 4th century. A near-by well contained pottery dated to A.D. 140–70. Some ditches of uncertain purposes were associated with both periods of occupation.[25] From a complex settlement on gravel land at Rectory Farm, Great Shelford (TL 447526), surface finds indicate an occupation extending from the neolithic to the Roman period. Here crop-marks indicate a palimpsest of rounded, sub-rectangular, and rectangular enclosures, ditch alignments, and groups of pits, some of which are aligned. With the Roman element perhaps indicated by rectilinear enclosures there seems no doubt that occupation was continuous from Iron Age into Roman times. Excavations have examined the boundary ditch of a field, with its associated palisade trench, which acted as a drain and from which came pottery of the 1st and 2nd century. Building debris indicated a structure somewhere in the area. The outer ditches may have served as field boundaries and with the associated droves there appear

[20] R.C.H.M. *Cambs.* ii. 71–3 and fig. 70.
[21] Fox, *Arch. Camb. Region*, 203; cf. R.C.H.M. *Cambs.* ii. 73 (no. 30) and fig. 60.
[22] R.C.H.M. *Cambs.* ii. 73 (no. 31) and fig. 58.
[23] Ibid. 81 (no. 30).
[24] Ibid. 62 (no. 37) and fig. 60.
[25] D. A. White, in *Proc. C.A.S.* lvi–lvii (1964), 30–41.

to have been two phases of the plan. Quarry or rubbish pits of the 2nd century were also excavated.[26]

Many new sites have come to light in south Cambridgeshire, some of which may have been connected with villas. At Girton (TL 423613) the field-ditches of an Iron Age settlement have been excavated, and there is a palimpsest of irregular field systems of the native type at Gamlingay (TL 219518), an area of sparse settlement. Between Kneesworth and Melbourn enclosures of Iron Age and Roman type may indicate another instance of continuity in occupation. Roman settlement has long been attested by stray finds near the Bran Ditch and a clearer view has been given of its extent from aerial photographs of an area south of Black Peak, Melbourn (TL 405444), revealing a fairly compact grouping of roughly rectangular enclosures, with straight droves leading towards a circular feature, perhaps an earlier and unrelated ring ditch. The settlement's relationship with the Bran Ditch is not clear, although traces of the Roman occupation on both sides of the ditch suggest that the ditch was cut through the settlement. In a belt of intensive settlement, both prehistoric and Roman, on the Rhee gravels from Shepreth to Harston, are complexes of linked rectangular and sub-rectangular enclosures of various sizes, with tracks and enclosures for individual dwellings. A large concentration lies north-west of Fowlmere (TL 415470) on either side of a stream running to the Rhee. The settlement south-west of the stream has the distinctive drove leading to pastures alongside the stream. Enclosures in the valley of the Hoffer brook, where a villa is known, are more dispersed. Further east Roman and earlier enclosures are found at Chronicle Hills, Whittlesford (TL 452476). In that area the spring-line had an important bearing on the location of the settlements.

Among other settlements evident on aerial photographs is a compact settlement of regular enclosures and droves at Old Drift, Fulbourn (TL 499569). The relationship of settlement to Wool Street has already been noted. At Yole Farm, Balsham (TL 57604935), there is a probable Roman farm north of Wool Street, and on the same side are some fairly compact and linked rectangular enclosures at Gunner's Hall, Balsham (TL 546512).

A few small settlements similar in layout to those on the gravels are found on the chalk at Balsham (TL 570518) and West Wratting (TL 576533), but the south-east part of the county appears to have been sparsely settled; some new finds have been made, for example at Todd's Farm, Dullingham (TL 61855820), where there is a settlement of fairly compact rectangular enclosures.

Although difficult to establish, a continuity of ownership from pre-Roman at least into the early Roman period may reasonably be inferred. The Boudiccan catastrophe may have affected some areas, while there is evidence for immigration in the late 1st century. Few details of continuity from Belgic times are known from the Belgic and Roman settlement at Abington Pigotts (TL 30104515), where occupation lasted throughout the Roman period.[27] Similar continuity is attested at Haslingfield and Orwell and by excavation in the grounds of the Plant Breeding Institute, Trumpington.[28]

At the other end of the Roman period it is clear that early English settlements were close to if not directly on the sites of Roman settlement. An example is Girton, while at Barrington the abandoned Roman settlement was used as a burial ground.[29] The

[26] J. K. S. St. Joseph, in *Antiquity*, xxxix (1965), 143–5; Alexander, Excavation Rep. 1975–6.

[27] G. F. Pigott, in *Proc. C.A.S.* vi (1891), 309–12; Fox, in *Proc. Prehist. Soc. E. Anglia*, iv (1924), 211–33; also at Barrington: J. W. E. Conybeare, in *Proc. C.A.S.* x (1904), 434–40; C.A.S. *Rep.* 44, pp. cxvi–cxvii.

[28] Orwell: unpublished surface finds; Trumpington: I. Davidson and G. J. Curtis, in *Proc. C.A.S.* lxiv. 1–14; cf., for the Ouse Valley, Green, in *Arch. News Letter*, vol. 5, no. 2, 29–32.

[29] W. K. Foster, *Proc. C.A.S.* v (1886), 5–32.

traces of Roman settlement on the sites of deserted medieval villages, as at Clopton and Childerley, may illustrate coincidence rather than continuity.[30]

AGRICULTURE

ROMAN farmers produced foodstuffs for one or more of four purposes, personal consumption, exchange in the market, payment of rent, and taxation. Most of the evidence for Roman agriculture within the county comes from the fenlands. Stukeley was the first to suggest that the fenlands were a granary for the Roman army in northern Britain, artificial watercourses providing a means of transport to the northern frontier.[1] Evidence obtained recently for the forms and scale of settlement indicates that cereal production was probably not a significant part of the economy, other than for local consumption. There was not enough land available to produce the large amounts of grain required by the Roman army. The canals may nevertheless have been important for transport. Indeed those in the north-east which link the fens with other parts of East Anglia may well have been important for the transport of grain. Further south the chalklands are excellent for barley and the villa estates along the fenland skirt may have produced barley, although those lands are also especially suitable for sheep rearing, which may have been more important during the late Roman period.

It has been suggested that the Wyboston type of settlement signifies a cattle and arable economy, while the larger rectangular fields of the St. Ives type indicate the production of cereals. Enclosures in the siltlands, covering only small areas and linked closely to the habitations, may represent stockyards and gardens. Long boundaries and droves point to the ranching of cattle, sheep, and horses. At War Ditches, Cherry Hinton, bones of cattle increase markedly in the Roman period, and it would appear that sheep declined from their relative importance in the economy of the early Iron Age. Cattle seem to have been especially important in the fens, while pigs by contrast are very rare. In the early Roman period, however, sheep were the main livestock on the siltlands, where they could have been grazed on the dry salt-marshes, free from the danger of fluke. It has been suggested that the later predominance of cattle resulted from an officially organized expansion of settlement involving the exploitation of wetter pastures. Those pastures, where sheep would have been exposed to fluke, could provide summer grazing and winter fodder for cattle.[2]

Cattle provided meat, hides, milk, and bone, and served as draught animals. Many of the products from cattle-raising may have been exported to the army in the north, notably leather, for which it had a huge demand, and salt beef, although beef could have been sent on the hoof. The unusually large number of cheese-presses found on fenland sites may reflect the importance of dairying.[3] Mutton and lamb were not highly prized in Roman times, and sheep were valued mainly for their wool and milk for making cheese. The high proportion of bones from older animals appears to bear this out, while the occurrence of loom-weights in some sites indicates that ready-made cloth

[30] *Medieval Arch.* v (1962), 333–4; vi–vii (1964), 341; Deserted Medieval Village Research Group, 9th Rep. 9; 12th Rep. 13–14; R.C.H.M. *Cambs.* i. 47. Pagan Saxon remains have been found at Clopton.

[1] For the significance of the Car Dyke see W. Stukeley, *Medallic Hist. of Marcus Aurelius Carausius* (1757), 125; Fox, *Arch. Camb. Region*, 180. Among recent discussions of the thesis see Salway and Hallam, in *Roman Fenland*,

13–14, 63, on whose work this section is largely based.

[2] Salway and Hallam, in *Roman Fenland*, 13–14, 63–4. Excavations at Golden Lion inn, Stonea, Wimblington (TL 460934), have revealed a high proportion of bird bones among animal remains with very few pigs: cf. *Roman Fenland*, 219. The over-all picture from the site appears to confirm the importance of cattle as a source of food. [3] Cf. Hartley, in *Roman Fenland*, 168.

may have been supplied to the army.[4] Horses were reared, probably also for supply to the army, although some were certainly eaten locally.

The production of cereals in the fens is indicated by the palaeobotanical record. At Cottenham a marked increase has been observed in the pollen of the weeds of cultivation.[5] From other areas threshing debris indicates a local production of cereals, notably spelt and hulled barley, the predominance of the former being in accord with the generally reported Roman preference. Before threshing the crop was dried, and a corn drying kiln has been found in the extreme south at Heydon Hill (TL 433408), although when excavated in 1848 its purpose was not understood. The kiln was revealed to be rectangular with walls of clunch, and amongst the debris were found, along with other objects, a bronze bell, cattle bones, and a coin of Constantius II (337–61).[6] Straw from cereals was used for tempering 'vessels' and the supports used in the preparation of salt.[7]

The fens and the valleys to the south produced also natural harvests. Of fish, a pike's jaw was found at War Ditches, Cherry Hinton,[8] while eels, popular in Anglo-Saxon times, are likely among other varieties to have been an important freshwater fish for the Romans also. Oyster-shells found on sites of all periods throughout the county probably represent local produce. Products of the fens include wildfowl, reeds and foliage for winter fodder, thatch, and peat which was used both for domestic and industrial fuel and also for walls and roofs. In addition to wool combs, the Worlington (Suff.) hoard (TL 684739) included reed-cutters of a type similar to those used at a later date.[9] Fen clay was an obvious source for daub, mud block, and pise.

The results of close study of the field systems in south Lincolnshire may reasonably be applied to the similar fenlands in the north of the county.[10] More than half of the fields have an area of less than 0·2 ha., and two-thirds less than 0·3 ha. The mean length is between 18·5 and 30 metres, and the breadth usually between 40 and 80 per cent of the length. Apart from such short rectangular 'Celtic fields' there are a few examples of the very long strip fields, which may be connected with a specialized technique in ploughing. The average ditched area for each settlement of the Wash sites seems to be c. 45 ha. (c. 110 acres).[11] In the 2nd century that indicates c. 20 ha. for each household. Given an average household of five, the allotment was c. 4 ha. (10 acres) for each head of population. Sixty per cent of the total area belonging to a settlement was not ditched, so that the total holding for the average settlement was just over 111 ha. (275 acres) or c. 50 ha. for each household.

Among the few agricultural implements known in the county, a scythe from Abington Piggotts came from the same workshop as the twelve in the well-known 4th-century hoard from Great Chesterford, indicating perhaps a pattern of distribution from the local market. There is no way of deducing whether the tools were made locally or imported. Also from Abington Piggotts has come a large plough-coulter of Romano-British type, indicating that a modest sophistication in agricultural techniques was accessible to the small farmer, who was probably of native stock. Other plough coulters are known from Fincham Farm, Wimblington (TL 465927), and, from just outside the county, from Hockwold cum Wilton (Norf.) (TL 710882).[12]

[4] Hallam, in *Roman Fenland*, 64.
[5] Applebaum, in *Agrarian Hist.* i (2), 206.
[6] Neville, in *Arch. Jnl.* ix (1852), 226; *Jnl. Brit. Arch. Assoc.* [1st ser.], iii (1848), 340; iv (1849), 76.
[7] Hallam, in *Roman Fenland*, 63.
[8] Hughes, in *Proc. C.A.S.* x (1904), 378.
[9] In Mildenhall museum; cf. *Roman Fenland*, 236.
[10] Hallam, in *Roman Fenland*, 64–7.

[11] Not much different from the holding of 200 *jugera* (50 ha.) mentioned by Columella, *De re rustica* II, xii. 7; cf. *Roman Fenland*, 85 n. 119.
[12] Applebaum, in *Agrarian Hist.* i (2), 86–7. For plough-coulters see Camb. Mus. (Abington Piggotts); *Roman Fenland*, 219 (Fincham Farm), 246 (Hockwold cum Wilton).

Appendix: Salt Production

Salt production in the fenlands has recently been treated in detail. The place named Salinae listed by Ptolemy among the Catuvellauni has been located, not necessarily correctly, in the Wash. Some industrial sites belong to the earliest phase of settlement in the fens, and the availability of salt may have been a primary motivation for the first settlers. Production seems largely to have ceased by the mid 2nd century, perhaps because ready supplies of the peat used for fuel were exhausted. Salt was used in the Roman period for the preservation of hides and mutton, birds, pork, fish, and oysters. How the industry was organized is not known but perhaps the Catuvellauni (if they were indeed the inhabitants) were permitted to operate through a system of concessions arranged with the provincial authorities.[13]

Brine was evaporated and dried using shallow clay-lined pits and trenches. Salt production seems to have been the principal activity at the sites but it is possible that ordinary pottery also was made along with the impermeable vessels required for boiling. On the surface the remains of the salt industry appear as patches of elevated ground composed of red soil. They are not usually associated with domestic remains, which are, however, occasionally found close by. The remains themselves comprise vessels, supports, and lining material, together with the baked clay surviving from the breakup of the supports and linings. The vessels were made in oxidized baked clay, 0·8 to 1·2 cm. thick, and were tempered with spelt straw. Some were probably nearly cylindrical in form but most have the shape of a deep tray formed by curving upwards the edges of a flat rectangle. Since the rectangular vessels were permeable, and therefore unsuitable for the boiling, they were used for drying. The supports take various forms: stands to support the vessels consisted of cylinders in rough clay but there are not many examples of the clay crossbars.

Among the sites of salt production, at Norwood, March (TL 418984), there are saltern pits, briquetage, fire-bars, and a cylindrical stand of baked clay. At Flaggrass, March (TL 434985), there are fire-bars that could come from kilns but which equally may have belonged to salt-working. Linings of burnt clay, clay supports, vessels, and slabs containing much vegetable matter have there been associated with salt production. At Coldham Hall, Elm (approx. TF 442022), there are saltern remains, including four clay cones, clay wedges, stands, bar fragments, and irregular squeezes. Other sites which have yielded similar remains include Laddus Drove, Elm (TL 473025), Stag's Holt, Elm (TL 435005), Wateringhill Farm east, Manea (TL 479926), Stonebridge Farm, Wimblington (TL 462942), and King's Delph, Whittlesey (TL 233954).[14]

CURRENCY

Circulation of Coinage

THE chronological distribution of coins found in the Cambridge region illustrates, or provides additional evidence for, the economic activity of the region in Roman times. A recent analysis of coins found throughout Lowland Britain[1] assigned each coin to one of 21 periods corresponding with imperial reigns (or groups or parts of reigns),

---

[13] Hallam, in *Roman Fenland*, 67–70. The location of Ptolemy's *Salinae* remains uncertain, and may be an error for Droitwich (Worcs.): see above, p. 5.
[14] *Roman Fenland*, 188, 219–21, 318–19, 322; Hallam, in

Lincs. Archit. and Arch. Soc. viii (1960), 74 (Flaggrass).
[1] R. Reece, in *Britannia*, iii (1972), 269–76; iv (1973), 227–51. The percentages exclude Roman coins found in Saxon cemeteries, coins found in hoards, and gold coins.

and was used to establish the number of coins, expressed as a percentage of the total, belonging to each period.[2] A similar analysis of 1,073 coins found in the Cambridge region yields percentage figures which may be compared with those for the whole of Lowland Britain.[3]

In the region the relatively high percentage of coins of period I (before A.D. 41)

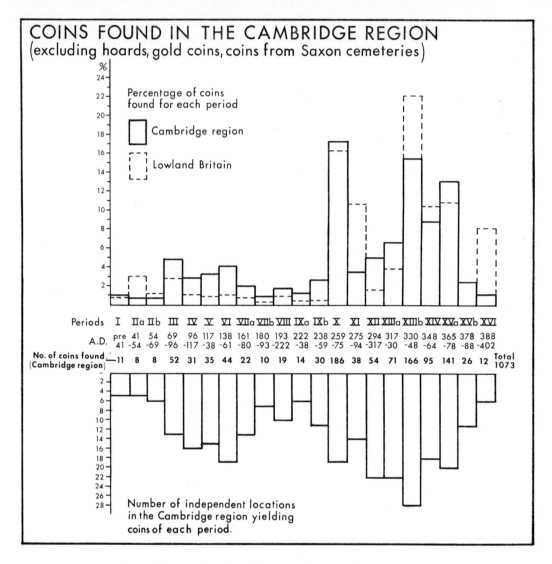

suggests a greater dependence than in other regions during period IIa (A.D. 41–54) on pre-Claudian silver, a suggestion which is strengthened by the region's strikingly low percentage, only a quarter of that for Lowland Britain, of coins of period IIa. At that time the major source of coins was perhaps the army, based from time to time at Great Chesterford, Godmanchester, and Cambridge, whence come seven of the eight Claudian coins recorded. A similarly low percentage in period IIb (A.D. 54–69) may reflect an economic stagnation accentuated by the aftermath of the Boudiccan rebellion.

[2] The following reigns are divided between more than one period: Gallienus (IXb–X), Salonina (IXb–X), Diocletian (XI–XII), Maximian (XI–XII), Allectus (XI–XII), Licinius (XII–XIIIa), Constantine I (XII–XIIIb), Constantine II Caesar (XIIIa–XIIIb), House of Constantine (XIIIa–XIV), Constantius II Caesar (XIIIa–XIIIb), Constans (XIIIb–XIV), Constantius II (XIIIb–XIV), Urbs Roma (XIIIb–XIV), Gratian (XVa–XVb), Theodosius I XVb–XVI), House of Theodosius (XVb–

XVI). Where coins which are assigned to a particular ruler by name cannot easily be placed in a period they are divided between the periods in proportion to the relative lengths of the periods, not in proportion to the relative numbers of coins that can be accurately placed in a period.

[3] The omission of the fenlands from the analysis is thought unlikely to invalidate for the whole county the conclusions based on the evidence drawn from the Cambridge region.

The relatively high percentage of Flavian coins (A.D. 69–96) is perhaps a measure of the local revival resulting from the official stimulus, recorded by Tacitus, during the governorship of Cn. Julius Agricola (A.D. 78–84). The even greater differences in percentages between the Cambridge region and Lowland Britain in periods IV and V reflect the economic expansion of the region in the 2nd century, when proportionately more coins circulated in the region than elsewhere in the province. In the Flavian and Antonine periods together (A.D. 69–180) the Cambridge region reveals a markedly higher percentage of coins (17·15) than Lowland Britain (6·49), representing rapid local development. The increase in settlement, especially on the fenland edges, reached a peak in the late 2nd century. There may have been a quick recovery from the Boudiccan rebellion and a sharp increase in population. Certainly the money economy was greatly enlarged. The sustained higher percentages in the Cambridge region in periods VIIb–IXb are remarkable in the light of the economic decline which is known to have affected the region, especially the fenlands. From the evidence presented in the graph for periods X–XVI (A.D. 259–402), in which some doubts arise from the difficulty of assigning coins to periods, two conclusions seem to be justified. First, the over-all percentage of coins is lower in the Cambridge region than in Lowland Britain. Secondly, the lower percentage may reflect the abnormally high level of circulation in the earlier periods rather than a low level of circulation compared with Lowland Britain as a whole, from the mid 3rd century onwards.[4]

The restricted use of coins until the late 1st century, against a political background which has already been considered, is clear from the graph showing the number of sites yielding coins of each period. If the coins of one period are assumed to have been used and deposited during the next,[5] an increase in circulation began under Trajan (A.D. 98–117) and reached a peak in the third quarter of the 2nd century, coinciding with the maximum growth of settlement. The relative decline that followed may represent local problems or an inadequate supply of new coins from official sources; the retention in use of older coins is a factor that the graphs cannot depict. On the same assumption about the length of time for which each coin circulated, the graph shows a return in the last quarter of the 3rd century to the level of circulation reached in the mid 2nd, followed perhaps by a slight depression that may have been caused by difficulties of coin supply rather than by general economic conditions. From c. A.D. 320 circulation climbed to a level beyond the 2nd-century peak, reaching a new maximum in the third quarter of the 4th century, a period of renewed economic activity reflected in artefacts and new settlements. It is to be remembered that the graph presents evidence of the distribution of single coins regardless of their value: since one 1st-century *sestertius* was the equivalent of 32 4th-century fourth bronzes (each half the weight of a *quadrans* which formed one-sixteenth of a *sestertius*), the prosperity of the mid 4th century evinced by a large number of coins is likely to have fallen far short of the level in the 2nd century, when the fewer coins known to have circulated were of greater value.

Coin Hoards

Coins were hoarded at different periods for a variety of reasons, but there are points in the history of Roman Britain when large numbers of coins were hoarded in different places at about the same time, attesting a widespread insecurity and lack of confidence

---

[4] Particular difficulties are posed by allusions in early excavation reports to 'many coins of the lower empire' and the like without further detail. As in Lowland Britain generally the supply of coins reached a peak in the mid 4th cent. The low percentage for period XVI in the Cambridge region contrasts with the evidence of fenland hoards for continued circulation into the 5th cent.

[5] Cf. Reece, in *Britannia*, iv. 249.

caused by the threat of incursions or economic decline. The late 3rd century was such a period, against a background of recorded disruption in both Britain and Gaul. The years 270–82 are especially prolific in hoards, when there is also a noticeable concentration in the eastern part of Britain, reflecting perhaps the threat to what was later to be known as the Saxon Shore.[6]

Cambridgeshire has yielded several hoards of that period. A hoard of 44 coins from Shelford contains 4 of Claudius II, 1 of Gallienus, 18 of Victorinus, 6 of Tetricus I, and 1 of Tetricus II, along with others not identified. The latest coins belong to the years A.D. 270–3.[7] From an unidentified location at Stonea, in Wimblington (approx. TL 4593), it is recorded that there was found 'nearly half a peck of base silver of the time of Gallienus', which might be identified with another find from a similar locality of 'coins of Gallienus and a silver vase, found 1820'.[8] Two hoards from Flaggrass, March (TL 434985), each contained 15 coins, ending with Gallienus and Postumus.[9] One from Hill Farm, Littleport (TL 538919), has a series ending A.D. 269–70 and at Linwood Farm, March (TL 408938), a group was hoarded about A.D. 270.[10] A large hoard of about 2,000 bronze coins from Gallienus to the Tetrici was found at Stonea Grange, Wimblington (TL 448937).[11] At Coldham Bank north, Elm (approx. TF 452022), a hoard of Antoniniani found in a pot over leaves contained 4 coins of Tetricus I, another possibly of the same emperor, another of either him or Postumus, 1 of Victorinus, and 1 of Claudius Gothicus.[12] The hoarding of such meagre sums of money suggests a relatively impoverished community with limited cash, or might indicate that such hoards were votive rather than emergency caches. Also from the period 270–5 is one hoard, or possibly two, from Newton (approx. TF 4314),[13] and from the Bungalow, Over (TL 386702), comes a deposit of slightly later date (c. 285).[14] Two more hoards can also be placed in the late 3rd century, one from Stonea Camp, Wimblington (TL 448931), another from Calves' Field, Wisbech St. Mary (TF 398057).[15]

Uncertainty in the region seems to have persisted into the reign of Constantine, although the number of hoards decreases, perhaps a reflection of growing confidence as the government sought to re-create security and re-establish the economy. The hoard from Middle Fen, Willingham (TL 405719), belongs to the very late 3rd century or the early 4th.[16] Also attributed to the early 4th century is a find in the bed of an extinct stream at New Mill, Isleham (TL 625790).[17] Two certain Constantinian coin hoards are known, one from Fen Causeway, Upwell (TL 4997), consisting of two pots containing coins of Constantine, the other deposited in a metal box at Over (TL 3770).[18]

The last years of the 4th century were particularly unsettled and it is not surprising to find several hoards of that date. At Elm (TF 4706) there was deposited a hoard

---

[6] Frere, *Britannia*, 215.   [7] Camb. Mus. acc. 33. 504.
[8] Babington, *Ancient Cambs.* 72; Fowler, in *Proc. C.A.S.* xliii. 16; cf. *Roman Fenland*, 219.
[9] *Roman Fenland*, 221.
[10] Fowler, in *Proc. C.A.S.* xliii. 7–13, 16; cf. *Roman Fenland*, 218, 231; Anne S. Robertson, in *Num. Chron.* 5th ser. xv (1935), 57; cf. C. H. V. Sutherland, *Coinage and Currency in Roman Britain*, 52 n. 3, 159.
[11] Babington, *Ancient Cambs.* 87; Fox, *Arch. Camb. Region*, 230; Robertson, in *Num. Chron.* 5th ser. xix (1939), 177; cf. H. Mattingly and J. W. E. Pearce, in *Bull. Bd. Celtic Stud.* ix (1939), 168; Fowler, in *Proc. C.A.S.* xliii. 16; cf. *Roman Fenland*, 218–19.
[12] *Proc. C.A.S.* lvi–lvii. 124 sqq.; cf. *Roman Fenland*, 320.

[13] Wm. Watson, *Hist. Wisbech* (1827), 487; Babington, *Ancient Cambs.* 89; Fowler, in *Proc. C.A.S.* xliii. 16; cf. *Roman Fenland*, 324.
[14] Walker, in *Proc. C.A.S.* xiv. 176 and map; cf. *Roman Fenland*, 191.
[15] *Roman Fenland*, 218 (Stonea Camp); *Wisbech Mus. Rep. 1950–1*, 7; cf. *Roman Fenland*, 298.
[16] Babington, *Ancient Cambs.* 86, mentions 'House of Constantine', although such issues do not appear in the published list of 500 coins found in a pot, cf. F. J. H. Jenkinson, *Proc. C.A.S.* v (1886), 225; *Roman Fenland*, 205.
[17] *Roman Fenland*, 237.
[18] Babington, *Ancient Cambs.* 74, 82; Fowler, in *Proc. C.A.S.* xliii. 17; *Roman Fenland*, 233 (Fen Causeway).

probably of the late 4th century.[19] A solidus of Theodosius was found in an indented Castor beaker enclosed within an oak box at Stonea Grange (TL 448945).[20] From the Arbury Road site was recovered a hoard of 17 coins associated with a fragment of a bronze ring and a green composition bead. The coins comprised 1 House of Constantine, 1 Magnentius, 4 barbarous imitations of the FEL. TEMP. REPARATIO type, 1 overstruck, and the rest minims. The excavator dated its deposition to *c.* A.D. 400 from the degree of wear.[21] Bronze coins found in a pot at Waldersea, Elm (TF 4403),[22] comprised mainly issues of Valentinian I, Arcadius, and Theodosius I. Two finds in Wisbech St. Peter are of similar date: 17 coins in a pot ended with Honorius and Arcadius (TF 4609) and 9 which possibly belonged to a hoard range from Constans to Arcadius (TF 4509).[23]

Rather later is the important hoard from Tiled House Farm, Stretham (TL 52327298), which indicates some sort of villa life persisting well into the 5th century. More than 865 coins were found in a pot, consisting of 9 radiates, 26 Constantinian, 35 Constantian, 45 Valentinian, and 649 Theodosian, deposited, according to one view, 'not earlier than the third decade of the 5th century'.[24]

The earliest hoard so far recorded comes from the March area (TL 4195) and, although there are doubts about the details, dates from the Hadrianic period.[25] Several depositions belong to the later 2nd century. Although the last years of the century were certainly far from tranquil there is little evidence that the Cambridge region was affected by the troubles of the north. A hoard at Doddington (TL 4190) contained coins from Vespasian to Antoninus Pius.[26] In a third hoard from Flaggrass (TL 434985) the last certain coin dates to A.D. 166–7.[27] At Horseheath silver coins found in a pot ranged in date from Nero to L. Verus and Marcus Aurelius, and a hoard of denarii from Knapwell ranged from Vespasian to Marcus Aurelius.[28] The latest coin in a deposit of gold and silver found at New Fordey Farm, Soham (TL 543752), is a first issue of Commodus of A.D. 180.[29] Rather later is what seems to have been a hoard of 23 so-called first and second brass coins from Domitian to Septimius Severus found in the Knapwell area.[30]

MATERIAL CULTURE

Trade

ALTHOUGH substantial quantities of objects furnish evidence in themselves for the movement of goods during the Roman period, discoveries illustrating such movement are scarce. In the fenlands there is reason to believe that the settlement at Flaggrass (TL 434985) served both as a centre for the local agricultural population and as a

[19] *Roman Fenland*, 324.
[20] *Arch. Jnl.* xix (1862), 365; cf. *Roman Fenland*, 218.
[21] Frend, in *Proc. C.A.S.* xlviii. 15, 40–3.
[22] Watson, *Wisbech*, 507; Fowler, in *Proc. C.A.S.* xliii. 14; cf. *Roman Fenland*, 320.
[23] Babington, *Ancient Cambs.* 88; cf. *Roman Fenland*, 323–4.
[24] Pearce, in *Proc. C.A.S.* xxxix. 85–92; cf. *Roman Fenland*, 226–7. In a personal communication D. C. Shotter has drawn attention to the worn condition of late coins in fenland hoards (in Wisbech Mus.).

[25] *Roman Fenland*, 220.
[26] W. M. Stukeley, in *Surtees Soc.* lxxvi (1883), 30; Fox, *Arch. Camb. Region*, 229; cf. *Roman Fenland*, 218.
[27] Nine bronze coins found in 1950–1, *Wisbech Mus. Rep. 1950–1*, 6; cf. *Roman Fenland*, 221.
[28] Babington, *Ancient Cambs.* 35 (Horseheath); *Proc. C.A.S.* viii (1895), 390; C.A.S. *Rep.* 37, p. xiii.
[29] R. A. G. Carson, in *Num. Chron.* 6th ser. xx (1960), 237–9; cf. *Roman Fenland*, 228.
[30] C.A.S. *Rep.* 37, p. xiii.

market and depot for local trade in imported and locally manufactured goods. The many querns found there may all come from a single store, while the site is remarkable for the number and variety of artefacts, including pins, beads, brooches, bracelets, and glass.[1]

Among goods in transit the 24 Roman lamps at Glassmoor, Whittlesey (approx. TL 314954), may have belonged to a cargo travelling on a lighter along the now extinct waterway from King's Dyke and the Nene south of Whittlesey to the West Water (approx. TL 376967).[2] Similarly 20 unused pots found at Richmond Hall, Gorefield, in Leverington (TF 414118), most of which were stacked, appear to have been a consignment in transit.[3] The movement of bulky building materials is suggested by stone rubble and roof and hypocaust tiles found in the river Ouse at St. Ives (Hunts.), and the find of Barnack ragstone at Swaffham Bulbeck (TL 52666706) belongs to a barge cargo, seeming to confirm the existence of a direct link by water between the Cam and the Nene.[4]

Stone

Before considering building stone one may note the use of the many semi-precious stones for jewellery and personal ornament. One of two intaglios in sardonyx is a splendid piece,[5] possibly of the 2nd century B.C., found in a 1st-century context in the probable villa at Shepreth, with a muscular Eros sporting in a brilliant orange field. The second was set on a gold finger-ring, reported from a garden on the Gog Magog Hills.[6] A reddish brown cornelian bead, in the form of an octagonally faceted cigar-shaped cylinder, appears among the Webb collection from Litlington. A bead with oval profile and central perforation in clear quartz found at Haslingfield may be of Roman origin.

Most of the Roman objects in jet are ornaments (beads, armlets, and pins), although some objects in the hoard from the Hempsals, Willingham (TL 436706), may have served a votive purpose.[7] The beads from that site are simple ring-beads, while most of those from the child burial at Linton are cylindrical.[8] Armlets of a simple oval form and D-shaped section are known from Gravel Hill Farm, while a piece perhaps from Barrington may have been penannular with a ring-and-dot decoration.[9] Jet pins belong to the more common types, with faceted heads such as the example from Haslingfield. There is little evidence for the date of these jet objects, what little there is pointing to the period after the late 2nd century in accord with evidence for the industry at York, or for how the trade in jet was organized. Its original source was Whitby (Yorks. N.R.) and the principal industry was located at York, but how it reached the region is unknown. Although women and children were the main users, jet still belongs to the class of high-quality goods and is likely to have been enjoyed only by persons of substance.[10] In addition to the jet beads two amber beads of simple annular form were found in the hoard from the Hempsals, Willingham.[11]

[1] *Roman Fenland*, 221–2. [2] Ibid. 196.

[3] Fowler, in *Proc. C.A.S.* xliii. 15; cf. *Roman Fenland*, 324. Most of the vessels are colour-coated. No trace of any kiln or storage buildings was found near by.

[4] Green, in *Arch. News Letter*, vol. 5, no. 2, 30; cf. *Roman Fenland*, 189 (TL 322699); R.C.H.M. *Cambs.* ii, 112 (no. 77).

[5] See Plate VIIB.

[6] M. Henig, *Corpus of Roman Engraved Gemstones*, ii (B.A.R. 8 (ii), 1974), p. 113, app. 48 plate ser. A (Shepreth); Neville, in *Arch. Jnl.* xi (1854), 212 (Gog Magog). An intaglio in amber cornelian comes from Milton Road,

Cambridge: Henig, *Roman Gemstones*, ii, p. 38, no. 247 plate ser. A.

[7] M. Rostovtzeff, in *J.R.S.* xiii (1923), 91 sqq.; cf. *Roman Fenland*, 209–10.

[8] See p. 90.

[9] Babington, in *Proc. C.A.S.* ii (1864), 289–92 (Gravel Hill); Camb. Mus. (Barrington). For the common types of jet pins, cf. R.C.H.M. *Eboracum* (1962), 143 and plate 69.

[10] A nearer centre of jet-working may have been Leicester: *Britannia*, iv (1973), 49.

[11] *Roman Fenland*, 209–10. The source of amber was the south shore of the Baltic.

The only objects known of shale are bracelets, roughly circular with D-shaped section, and whorls; the whorls, like those from Fen Ditton, are circular discs with bevelled edges, whose purpose remains a puzzle.[12]

The use of a variety of stone for building is attested by discoveries throughout the region. The quarries of Barnack (Northants.) stone lie 5 km. south-east of Stamford, where more than one type of the stone was worked. Apart from a freestone bed of shelly oolite and a shallow bed of ragstone, the main deposit is a deep bed of coarse-textured and shelly limestone, the Barnack rag hardstone used extensively in the Roman period. The expense of working it restricted its use to the buildings and coffins of the wealthy. Masonry described as 'hammer-dressed Barnack rag' was found at Swaffham Bulbeck (TL 52616725), perhaps belonging to a cargo in transit during the 1st century, and it is recorded at Cambridge in the 4th-century defences. Several other references to Northamptonshire limestone may denote Barnack (see below). It appears to have been especially suitable for coffins which were apparently delivered in the finished condition. Most probably the stone, which is found as far away as London, reached the Cambridge region by water, probably along the Welland, the Lincolnshire Car Dyke, Cnut's Dyke, the former course of the Ouse (West Water) from Benwick to Earith, in Bluntisham (Hunts.), and the Cambridgeshire Car Dyke (Old Tillage) to the Cam.[13]

The quarries of Ketton (Rut.) limestone lie in the same area as those of Barnack, a little further west. This good stone was used for the Comberton villa and in the basilican building at Ickleton.[14] Its best known appearance in the region is at Girton where what may be the remains of a funerary monument includes a sculpture of a lion devouring a deer or calf, set on a rectangular plinth. Other fragments from the same panel include the lion's paws and other limbs. The animal's face is naturalistically carved and the mane shown conventionally as banks of curls. Perhaps it was the work of a sculptor in the area near the quarries.[15] In the same area as Barnack and Ketton lie the quarries of Collyweston (Rut.) stone, a thinly bedded stone especially suitable for roof tiles, for which it was used extensively during the Roman period in Cambridge (Castle Hill). Slates of Stonesfield or Collyweston stone were used in the Ickleton villa, and a similar slate has been found on the surface at Chronicle Hills, Whittlesford (TL 452476).[16]

Among stones probably from Barnack or Ketton the sculptured male torso from Girton had a belted tunic[17] and a head (lost) carved separately. It may come from a tombstone. Among fragments from Arbury Road, Cambridge, are the lower right thigh and knee of a life-size figure from a 4th-century pit (site I) and another fragment which may represent drapery.

From the same settlement a sculptured panel which belonged to the aisled building of the 2nd and 3rd centuries depicts an armed figure standing within a niche; since it has a shield and spear the figure may represent a war-god. The style is markedly provincial and it may have been executed in a local workshop. Of four fragments of frieze or cornice one has the head of a young male in three-quarter relief; in spite of the poor stone the standard of execution is higher than normal for the area, as exemplified in

---

[12] The shale came from the Isle of Purbeck in Dorset; cf. R.C.H.M. *Dorset*, ii (3), 524–5. The products entered the region in Belgic times. Waste cores in Camb. Mus. may come from Trumpington, but the many examples in the Braybrooke collection are probably not of local origin. Both finished objects and unworked shale may have reached the region during the Roman period.

[13] D. Purcell, *Camb. Stone* (1967), 29–34 (Barnack quarries); R.C.H.M. *Cambs*. ii. 112 (no. 77) (Swaffham Bulbeck); above, p. 42 (Cambridge); Green, in *Arch. News Letter*, vol. 6, no. 12 (1955), 276 (London); below, p. 89 (coffins).

[14] Babington, *Ancient Cambs*. 23 (Comberton); Fox, *Arch. Camb. Region*, 184 (Ickleton).

[15] For the Girton sculptures, now in Camb. Mus., see Edith J. Hollingworth and Maureen M. O'Reilly, *Anglo-Saxon Cemetery at Girton Coll., Camb.* (1925); cf. Jocelyn M. C. Toynbee, *Art in Britain under the Romans* (1964), 114. See below, Plate VIIIc.

[16] Liversidge, *Britain in the Roman Empire*, 254 (Ickleton). See also Roach Smith, in *Jnl. Brit. Arch. Assoc.* [1st ser.], iv. 356.

[17] See Plate VIIIB.

another piece from the same site where the face in a gabled niche at an angle of the frieze is carved in the crudest fashion. The third is an angle block with a simple ovolo frieze in negative relief, and the fourth has a five-petal rosette in relief within a gabled frame across the angle between two planes.[18] A column-base in shelly yellow limestone was found at Carter's Well, Grantchester.[19] The only recorded use of Corallian stone from Upware is at Glebe Farm south-west, Willingham (TL 435714), although loads were transported along the Ouse to St. Ives, Houghton, and Somersham (all Hunts.).[20] Two instances of the probable use for building of chert, whose nearest source is Cottenham, occur at West Fen (TL 400722) and Middle Fen, Willingham (TL 402723).[21]

Various stones were used for other purposes than building. The fragment of a basin from Latham Road, Cambridge, is in a marble of unknown but probably Mediterranean origin.[22] Tesserae, many of limestone, from destroyed mosaics are often the sole trace of once well-appointed buildings. An unpublished study of tesserae from the villa at Burwell describes four different varieties of limestone, with others of tile, sandstone, and flint.[23] Tesserae of a greyish limestone are known from a number of major Roman sites, including Litlington, the Temple, Isleham, Landwade villa, and Chronicle Hills, Whittlesford. They and other varieties were perhaps made from local erratics of different limestones. Limestones provided other objects for structural or decorative purposes at Chronicle Hills, Landwade villa, and Burwell (TL 584675), and for a stone palette at Litlington villa. Spindle-whorls found at Wicken and Childerley were probably of local erratics, as is a polished slab in grey carboniferous limestone from Cambridge (Arbury Road), whose original source was probably North Yorkshire.[24]

The building stone most easily obtained locally was chalk clunch, of which a number of small quarries were worked in the Roman period, besides perhaps the much larger medieval quarries at Reach, where the building of the Lode in the Roman period may have been connected with exploitation of the clunch. In the Saxon cemetery at Burwell (TL 590665) a pit of Roman date 3·5 metres deep with a diameter of 5·5 to 6·0 metres at the top and 2·75 to 3·5 metres at the base had served as a mine for chalk used in a near-by structure.[25] A similar purpose, if not lime extraction, was served by a pit of the Antonine period at War Ditches, Cherry Hinton.[26] Limekilns probably of Roman date are known at Fulbourn railway station. The largest of three pits in the chalk was 2 metres deep with a diameter of 3 metres, then 2 metres diameter to a further depth of 1·25 metres, with an 8 cm. coating of cement and 20 cm. of fire-reddened concrete on the inner surface. The upper fill was calcareous, the lower carbonaceous. At the junction of upper and lower levels a passage 0·85 metre long connected with another pit, linked by a similar passage to the third pit. The last was not circular but had parallel sides with a floor that probably sloped up to the surface.[27]

The use of clunch for building is well attested, in structures such as at Burwell castle, Comberton villa, Ickleton villa, Heydon Hill corn-drying kiln, and Mutlow Hill barrow, and in Cambridge and at the Arbury Road settlement, where Melbourn rock was also used.[28] At Barrington blocks of clunch forming an ovolo moulding and in-

[18] See p. 44 and Plates VIIID, VIIIE.
[19] See Plate VIIIA. Porter, in *Proc. C.A.S.* xxii. 124–6. Some fluted oolite stones are recorded from Horseheath: Walker, in *Proc. C.A.S.* xv. 184.
[20] *Roman Fenland*, 210.   [21] Ibid. 205–6.
[22] Walker, in *Proc. C.A.S.* xv. 192–6.
[23] MS. by W. H. Foster of 1905 in Camb. Mus.
[24] For Arbury Road see p. 44.
[25] Lethbridge, in *Proc. C.A.S.* xxx (1929), 97–8; cf.

R.C.H.M. *Cambs.* ii. 41 (no. 129).
[26] White, in *Proc. C.A.S.* lvi–lvii. 9–41.
[27] J. Carter, in *Proc. C.A.S.* iii (1879), 313–15. Another near by was recorded by Hughes, in *Proc. C.A.S.* x. 177, where a stone-lined pit 4 metres deep was cut in two stages in similar fashion, with a flue and cross-flue at the bottom. At the bottom was found coked wood, fern, and a fill of burnt chalk which contained Roman pottery.
[28] Clare Fell, *Proc. C.A.S.* xlix (1956), 13–23.

corporated in the foundations of a water-mill may have come from a Roman building, perhaps that recorded in the adjoining field.[29] Chalk is also found used for tesserae at the Temple, Isleham, Chronicle Hills, Whittlesford, and Landwade. The spindle-whorl found on the Saxon cemetery at Burwell is probably Roman, while a small jar hollowed in chalk less than 5 cm. high from Cambridge (Castle Hill) may also be of Roman date. Like chalk, with which it is closely associated, flint occurs widely in the area and was used extensively for building, in the villas at Comberton, Ickleton, Landwade, and Reach, in structures at Cambridge, and for a tomb and the enclosure walls in the Litlington cemetery.

Most of the various sandstones used in the area were derived probably from local erratic sources. Tesserae are found at Landwade villa and Shepreth, and whetstones at Chronicle Hills, Whittlesford. A rubber possibly of Roman date from Hauxton mill and a mortar from Horningsea are also recorded. Sandstone querns are found in various settlements, including Arbury Road, and a palette, probably of sandstone, comes from the Litlington villa.

Gravels and other alluvial or drift sources were used extensively, gravels and cobbles especially for floors and yards. Pits at Cambridge reveal that large quantities of gravel were obtained locally. Examples of pebbles used as spindle-whorls are known from Haslingfield and Horningsea, and the gravels were also the source of schist whetstones, such as the example from Chronicle Hills, Whittlesford, while others of doubtful date came from Bourn and Cambridge (Magdalene College). A large rounded water-worn pebble from New Fordey Farm, Soham, may have been used as a rubber, while perhaps the most unusual objects are the hairpins made from belemnite fossils, said to have been discovered at Comberton villa.

Coal was certainly used in the region during the Roman period, presumably brought from the north, perhaps as ballast in barges. A layer of coal of a type obtained in Nottinghamshire and South Derbyshire was found sandwiched between two chalk and gravel layers of the *agger* of Wool Street, while a deposit was also found in the Car Dyke near Bullock's Haste.[30]

Quern stones for milling were obtained from well-known sources. Some made of the best quality Rhineland lava are known both in the fenlands and in the south, and their quantity and distribution are matched by more local products, such as those of Hertfordshire puddingstone. The upper stone of the latter variety is bun-shaped, with the lower stone somewhat flatter.[31] Querns in millstone grit are less common than those in sandstone, some of which may have been made from local erratic deposits. There are a few examples of the older saddle quern in sandstone, although most are of the rotary type. The 'beehive' querns of puddingstone from Abington Piggotts have been dated to the pre-Roman era, indicating perhaps a continuity in supply from Iron Age to Roman times.[32] The widespread discoveries of querns throughout the region suggest the importance of agriculture and cereal crops, although recent studies of the fenlands have placed greater emphasis on the role of cattle-rearing there.

Painted Plaster

As an indication of affluence the remains of rooms whose walls or ceilings were decorated with polychrome painted plaster can be most informative, although the

---

[29] Fox, *Arch. Camb. Region*, 183; C.A.S. *Rep.* 44, p. cxvi.

[30] I. A. Richmond, *Roman Britain*, 160 (ballast); Dewhurst, in *Proc. C.A.S.* lvi–lvii. 50 (Wool Street); *J.R.S.* xxxviii. 88–9 (Bullock's Haste).

[31] See E. A. Rudge, in *Trans. Essex Arch. Soc.* 3rd ser. i (1968), 247–9.

[32] Fox, in *Proc. Prehist. Soc. E. Anglia*, iv. 212; cf. Fox, *Arch. Camb. Region*, 108.

remains from the region are meagre and generally associated with villas or larger settlements. Proprietors who aspired to *Romanitas* possibly formed a very small minority of the population. Where painted plaster does occur it matches the standard found elsewhere in the province, as is demonstrated by the wall-paintings from the Ickleton villa where several rooms had panel schemes employing red, red and white with black stripes, blue, grey-blue dotted with yellow and red, yellow, and red and white. Within the panels were various designs, including fleurs-de-lis in scarlet, a herring-bone pattern in brown and black lines, and foliate designs in yellow ochre and green. The angle of one wall was adorned by a wild red rose, with green leaves on a white ground. One design, the gable-end of a building drawn in black on a brown background with a red roof, may belong to an idealized rural scene. Only the foot and some clothing, light green with a brown border, survives of a figure, perhaps a dancing nymph or maenad.[33]

Painted designs in the Arbury Road settlement (TL 455615) include linear bands, geometric and non-geometric floral motifs, and curvilinear patterns, in a wide range of colours including white, red-brown, scarlet, black, grey, light green, pink, brown, and cream.[34] One house on the Arbury Road site has produced fragments of a dado, with an area of simulated marble panelling. Higher on the same wall were panels in blue, light green, red, and white, with floral motifs in maroon and yellow.[35] Some of the painted plaster from the town of Cambridge comes from non-masonry structures; they included a range of floral motifs and curvilinear designs. The Landwade villa has produced wall-plaster painted in a great variety of colours, including white, yellow ochre, green, maroon, orange-brown, grey, black, pink, red, purple, yellow, and blue. The designs are of the familiar zonal types and there are also simulated marbling and floral motifs. Some pieces were curved, and probably come from mouldings around windows and doors, and in one instance the dado was offset from the upper wall by a chamfer.[36] Polychrome plaster is known also from Bullock's Haste, Burwell castle, Burwell Fen (TL 584675), Chronicle Hills (TL 452476), Latham Road, Grantchester, and the Temple, Isleham, and from villas at Bartlow, Comberton, Shepreth, and Reach.

Pottery

Any survey of the Roman pottery used in Cambridgeshire must remain for the most part provisional, although recent studies have made great advances.[37] Before the Flavian period pottery used in the region tends to bear out the conclusion that the whole area is conservative in its ceramic traditions. Vessels of the pre-Roman Belgic types predominate in the south, a feature already noted at Runcton Holme (Norf.).[38] Forms such as the narrow-mouthed carinated jar persisted much later in the region than elsewhere although during the middle of the 1st century a limited amount of South Gaulish samian and early Rhenish types appear, a consequence of the presence of the Roman army. The quantity of evidence increases in the Flavian and Trajanic period. Some small kilns, producing for local needs, are known at War Ditches, Milton, and Over. Moreover if the beakers decorated *en barbotine* and comparable vessels were made at War Ditches then some degree of sophistication had evidently developed in local taste. The potters may have been newcomers working in a wholly Roman tradition,

---

[33] *Jnl. Brit. Arch. Assoc.* [1st ser.], iv (1849), 361; cf. Liversidge, in *Proc. C.A.S.* xliv (1951), 13–17; *The Roman Villa in Britain*, ed. Rivet, colour plates 4. 1–2, 4. 5–6. See also Toynbee, *Art in Roman Britain* (1962), 195 no. 174.

[34] Excavated by Mr. M. F. Howard of Cambridge.

[35] Frend, in *Proc. C.A.S.* xlviii. 22.

[36] Some of the Landwade plaster is illustrated in *The*

Roman Villa in Britain, ed. Rivet, fig. 4. 5–6.

[37] While there remains much of value in Fox, *Arch. Camb. Region*, 200–13, the most important work is now the study of fenland pottery by K. F. and B. R. Hartley, in *Roman Fenland*, 165–9.

[38] See Hartley, in *Proc. C.A.S.* xlviii. 27; C. F. C. Hawkes, in *Proc. Prehist. Soc. E. Anglia* [1st ser.], vii (2) (1933), 231–62.

although older methods of production still continued to serve their more restricted market.

At that time the fenlands used pottery from several sources. Supplies to the east fenlands from near-by Norfolk continued throughout the 2nd century, while the west fenlands imported from factories in the Nene Valley, which produced calcite-gritted storage jars, cooking pots in a Belgic tradition, and platters imitating Gallo-Belgic forms. *Mortaria*, not made locally during the 1st century, were imported to the fenlands from sources in the area of Verulamium, although the quantity appears to have been very small. Perhaps the lack of *mortaria* from Kent and Colchester indicates that sea traffic by the Wash had not yet been organized. South Gaulish samian is found on fenland sites then occupied.

Under Hadrian the pattern of supply appears to have changed markedly throughout the area. In the south it was about then that Horningsea and neighbouring potteries began production, reaching a peak in the later 2nd century, continuing into the 3rd, until they succumbed to massive competition from the Nene Valley. Horningsea was perhaps the first pottery run on Roman commercial lines, and probably superseded more local centres. The development of Cambridge and the expansion of fenland settlement presumably created a new market which was supplied by Horningsea and other un-identified local kilns, although some pottery was still produced in older traditions. In the 2nd century Horningsea supplied the southern fenlands, Norfolk the east, and the Nene valley the west, with the last source dominating the entire market from the late Antonine period. It appears that very little pottery was obtained from further afield: no black burnished is known, and only a few vessels from the Verulamium area.[39]

When under Hadrian the Verulamium potteries declined to local production only, supplies of *mortaria* to the fenlands changed, the east drawing from Norfolk, the west from Hartshill and Mancetter (Warws.), probably via Leicester, and a lesser quantity from the East Midlands. Later in the 2nd century supplies were obtained from Colchester and in small quantities from the Nene Valley, which made a late start in the specialized *mortaria* market.[40] Most supplies of samian pottery came from the central Gaulish kilns at Lezoux (Puy-de-Dôme), although during the late 2nd and early 3rd centuries there is a higher proportion of east Gaulish products than average for the rest of Britain. From the same area were imported Rhenish colour-coated beakers, and in the Girton burial a rare instance of a lead-glazed vessel from the Rhône probably also came via the Rhineland.

The apparent scarcity of decorated samian suggests a low purchasing power in the region, and a rarity of imported amphorae and a general scarcity of flagons point to a preference for beer over wine. The numerous storage jars reflect the difficulties of pit storage in such a damp area. Cheese-presses occur frequently in the fenlands.[41]

In the 3rd century the fenlands were dominated by products of Nene Valley potteries, both coarse and colour-coated products, to an extent of more than 90 per cent. The predominance is less marked in the south, where local production continued. Few other imports are recorded: *mortaria* were now obtained almost exclusively from the Nene Valley, whence easy transport by water enabled that centre to take the market from the Warwickshire kilns. The same pattern continued into the 4th century, with some local production as the wasters from Jesus Lane, Cambridge, of the end of the 3rd or beginning of the 4th century indicate (although some date them to the 2nd century on the basis of their forms). Imported pottery now came from further south,

[39] *Roman Fenland*, 165–7.
[40] An example of a herring-bone stamped *mortarium* is known from Madingley Road.
[41] *Roman Fenland*, 168.

especially Oxfordshire, and the appearance of 'Romano-Saxon' pottery may reflect new tastes in design brought about by immigrants to the area. During the 3rd century most small-scale production of *mortaria* appears to have ceased, and most supplies came from Warwickshire, the Nene Valley, and Oxfordshire. The fenlands drew about three-quarters of their supplies from the Nene valley. In the late 4th century the red colour-coated *mortaria* from south-east Oxfordshire replaced the products of the Warwickshire kilns which had by then ceased production.

The pattern of pottery imports changed, therefore, during the Roman period on lines that seem general throughout south-east Britain. After an early self-sufficiency there are signs of an incorporation into networks of distribution devised for mass products from main centres over great parts of the province, with changes in product reflecting the rise and decline of the different centres.

Of local pottery production, evidence for one or more kilns at War Ditches, Cherry Hinton, came from the earliest excavations, when particular note was made of the barbotine ware, as well as debris which included grass-marked and probably straw-marked clay discs perhaps from a kiln dome as at Horningsea. An excavated kiln proved to be of the usual updraught type, built of clay, with a circular oven chamber 1 metre in diameter containing an elongated central pedestal, and with an unusually short flue passage. The fabric used was a micaceous, oxidized orange-brown to buff clay, decorated with regular and well executed rilling and scouring, with a fine burnish applied to the body. The pots are divided on basis of form into four types, which reflect a Belgic ancestry. Type 1, a large narrow-mouthed jar, accounts for less than 10 per cent of the production; type 2, a medium-mouthed jar in two sizes, accounted for about half the output; type 3 is a wide-mouthed jar accounting for about a quarter, and type 4, an imitation of Gallo-Belgic platters, was burnished on both sides, with three deeply incised concentric grooves representing the foot-ring. On general appearance they have been dated to the 1st century.[42]

Two pottery kilns, accompanied by debris and wasters, have been found at the gravel-pits near Milton (TL 482623). The kiln domes were made from the same fabric used for the products, which included coarse jars and dishes of the late 1st or early 2nd century. Of similar date were the dumps of clay firebars, clay debris, pottery, and wasters found at Cold Harbour Farm, Over (TL 393698).[43] The kilns at War Ditches, Milton, and Over, represent small-scale production in the early Roman period, perhaps on private estates, and probably served local needs only. Such individual kilns were replaced in the mid 2nd century by organized large-scale production yielding much larger quantities for a wider market. Perhaps earlier private kilns were made unworkable by mass production at one or two centres near the Cam and Car Dyke waterway.

During the 2nd century the Horningsea kilns (TL 497634) appear to have been

[42] Hughes, in *Proc. C.A.S.* x. 452–81; for kiln excavation see Lethbridge, ibid. xlii (1949), 120–1, 124 and plate XII; cf. Hartley, ibid. liii (1960), 23–8. The early date is supported by the absence of the products from the Humphries Road site, Cambridge. It is likely that the well-known barbotine ware was also produced at War Ditches: local distribution extended at least to the Guilden Morden cemetery. This pleasing and high-quality ware has a buff to cream fabric, and the typical vessel is a small beaker often with a cornice rim, decorated *en barbotine* with dot panels and dot and circle designs in red or brown. Perhaps it was the work of a skilled potter from elsewhere. The aisled house (see above, p. 31 n. 3) may indicate an exotic presence.

[43] *Roman Fenland*, 189, 200. Other places have produced evidence for the manufacture of pottery, although no reliable evidence for their date is available. A pottery kiln is reported at Coldham Bank north, Elm (TL 452021), and wasters from Maltmas Farm, Elm (TL 460037), may indicate a local pottery; cf. *Roman Fenland*, 320–1. A clay plate, which might have belonged to an oven or kiln, is recorded from Meadow Drove, Willingham (TL 433708). At Arbury Road a kiln not earlier than the 2nd cent., perhaps connected with the Humphries Road site, may be another example of an estate producing the coarsest wares for local needs.

a major source of pottery for the region. Evidence from Arbury Road suggests that production began a little before the mid 2nd century and reached a peak during the later 2nd century, with products spreading throughout the area and into Hertfordshire and Huntingdonshire.[44] The kilns take the form of a bowl-shaped hole lined with clay, with piers to support the firebars projecting from the lining around the edge. The flue was located on the west or north-west side and in some cases its junction with the body was an arched opening, with the floors of kiln and flue at the same level. The flue was a covered passage, 0·60 metres long and 20 cm. high built of puddled clay mixed with pottery and pieces of broken clay plates. (In other examples the flue arch was made by cutting away the kiln wall and plugging it with puddled clay to leave an opening c. 20 cm. high at the bottom.) In one kiln the mouth of the flue was forked into two. Three kilns appear to have belonged to a different type. They had regular arched flues but only four side-pillars, compared with the eight in others, and at the base were elongated almost to a diamond shape rather than the more usual circular form. Also noteworthy was the manner in which the upper wall of the kiln turned outwards at the edge to form a rim.[45]

The kilns were covered with domes, temporary and removable structures of brushwood, grass, straw, and reeds; over the domes were placed rounded clay plates from 0·15 to 0·25 metres across and 12–25 mm. thick, on which was deposited another layer of vegetation which was topped with earth and clay. Numerous clay plates carried impressions of the vegetation used, which included spelt, barley, tall oat grass, and meadow grass, although most widespread was threshed wheat and barley straw. Willow twigs and furze stems were used for fuel. In addition to the plates from the dome, rings and lumps of clay which may have served as pottery supports were also found. The most distinctive product of the Horningsea kilns appears to have been the large storage jar, often with double rim and a simple combed decoration, although other jars, bowls, and platters were also produced. Fabrics varied but the jars were made in a sandy grey to brown clay. A common form of decoration was point punctuation showing as linear designs of squarish indentations. Among other products wasters of indented beakers are known, while *mortaria* were probably made, besides miniatures, lids, and simple lamps.[46] Some bone pins from the site are thought to have been used for modelling.[47] One remarkable vessel made at Horningsea is a narrow-mouthed shouldered jar in brown colour-coated ware, with relief figures on the body, including a possible horse and a lion with ears and eyes painted white and mane and claws incised. Both are rendered in the Celtic style but unlike that of the Hunt cups. The bodies of the figures have been pressed out from inside while the outlines and details were tooled on the external surface.[48]

The wasters found near Jesus Lane, Cambridge, come probably from a kiln which

[44] Frend, in *Proc. C.A.S.* xlviii. 26 sqq. (Arbury Road). Hughes, ibid. x. 176, recorded dumps of wasters and a probable find of kilns by some workmen, and noted how suitable was the alluvial clay for pottery and the gault for brick and tile. Although not altogether satisfactory, the only detailed record of the kilns is Walker, ibid. xvii (1914), 14–70.

[45] In the main type of kiln the rim diameter varied from 1·6 to 2·3 metres, and the depth from rim to base between 0·55 to 0·95 metre, with a base width from 0·45 to 0·7 metre. Flue heights ranged from 0·45 to 0·6 metre, widths from 0·3 to 0·35, height of pillars 0·4 to 0·6, and diameter of pillar tops was from 0·25 by 0·2 to 0·45 by 0·3 metre. One kiln had three phases of use, ending as an exceptionally small structure. The excavator believed that it began by producing large jars but at the end produced only shallow saucers and bowls. In the second type of kiln the upper diameter ranged between 1·00 and 2·00, the base from 0·4 to 1·00, and the depth up to 1·00 metre. The flue slit was from 0·25 to 0·45. In one kiln the eight pillars were disposed in four pairs, 0·5 high with tops 0·2 metre in diameter but tapered almost to a point at the base.

[46] On the evidence of forms such as the pedestalled jars the beginning of Horningsea production was once assigned to the 1st cent., but local conservatism appears to have retained the older fashion into the late 2nd: Hartley, in *Proc. C.A.S*, liii. 28.

[47] C.A.S. *Rep.* 45, p. xxxii.

[48] Camb. Mus. acc. R. 212. The problem of the identity of the 'horse' arises from its horns, painted white. See PLATES IXA, IXB.

belonged to the settlement at St. Sepulchre's Hill and may exemplify the industrial nature of that part of Roman Cambridge. Formerly assigned to the 1st century the vessels have since been dated to the late 3rd or early 4th century and show that local factories could still operate in the face of competition from the Nene Valley. The fabric at Jesus Lane is grey and its products have been assigned to four different groups, on the evidence of form. Dating is based on parallels from Great Chesterford and Colchester.[49]

The role of imports in the pottery used in the region may be illustrated by a few well-known items of intrinsic interest. Apart from samian products other pottery was shipped directly from the Rhineland to the Wash, an example being the incense-burner of the early 2nd century in white ware from the Litlington cemetery, which has the name INDV(L)CIVS spelt out in perforations.[50] Drinking vessels with appropriate mottoes applied *en barbotine* come from Guilden Morden and Ickleton, the former with VTERE FELIX, the latter with [SI]C AMICI BIBVNT.[51]

Although some lamps were made locally the good-quality products came from the Mediterranean. A fine specimen from Ely belongs to the volute nozzle type of the 1st century A.D. and was a type given as a present at the new year, known from several parts of the Roman Empire. Within the discus a victory holds a palm branch in her left hand, and in her right a shield bearing the message ANNVM NOVVM FAVSTVM FELICEM MIHI, with the surrounding field occupied by sweets, nuts, cakes, bread, three coins with types of a two-headed Janus, two clasped hands, and a winged cupid.[52]

The familiar products of the Nene Valley are found throughout the area. More sporadically in early centuries, and constantly in the 4th century, the so-called calcite-gritted jars and bowls occur frequently, especially the later flanged varieties. The source may be the Nene Valley but other centres of production are suspected. Essex and Hertfordshire products remain for the most part an unknown quantity, although they may account for some of the early trade in the south and some sites in the far south may have lain within the trading orbit of Great Chesterford.[53] The label Upchurch Ware was once applied to imported wares from several sources, including poppy-headed beakers with patterns of raised dots forming rhomboi. Typical of the group are bowls imitating samian forms in polished black and grey fabric, decorated with incised vertical and horizontal lines and concentric semicircles. A fine specimen comes from War Ditches, Cherry Hinton.[54] The Suffolk kilns of West Stow are believed to have served some local needs, while a recurring feature in collections of 4th-century pottery is the red colour-coated Oxfordshire wares, notably bowls and *mortaria* with their characteristic stamped designs. They represent a local British attempt to meet the demand once satisfied by the samian products, which ceased to enter Britain after the earlier 3rd century.

Among the more specialized vessels one may note the 'baby's feeding bottle' from

---

[49] See Plate IXc. Hughes, in *Proc. C.A.S.* x. 194–6; cf. Fox, *Arch. Camb. Region*, 211. Redating and classification has been provided by Hartley, in *Proc. C.A.S.* liii. 26–7. Type 1 is a narrow-necked vessel, a flagon without handles, with a pedestal in two varieties. Most of the outside is coated with a silver-grey slip. Type 2 is a narrow-necked vessel of flagon form with the normal flagon base, a similar slip to type 1, and wavy lines on an unburnished band at the shoulder (on two of three examples). Type 3 is a wide-mouthed jar of similar fabric to types 1–2, but one piece has a black bituminous slip on the upper exterior. Type 4 may not have been made at the kiln. A single example, certainly not a waster, in form imitates Dragendorf

samian form 31 in an orange-brown fabric with red colour-coating.

[50] Fox, *Arch. Camb. Region*, 208; cf. ibid. plate XXI (3–3a).

[51] S. S. Lewis, in *Proc. C.A.S.* iv (1881), 337–41; Roach Smith, in *Jnl. Brit. Arch. Assoc.* [1st ser.], iv. 364. The lead-glazed globular jar with rilling from the 2nd-cent. burial at Girton probably has a Gallic origin.

[52] Liversidge, in *Proc. C.A.S.* xlvii (1954), 40 (Ely).

[53] The obscurity ought to be partly dispelled by a study of the pottery from Cambridge excavations.

[54] Fox, *Arch. Camb. Region*, 208; cf. ibid. plate XXII (1).

Latham Road, Cambridge.[55] Besides the unusually large number of cheese-presses already mentioned, colanders are also frequent throughout the region, from Bullock's Haste, Cottenham, the Stacks north, Willingham, and Abington Pigotts. Pottery fabric had several secondary uses. The spindle-whorl is common throughout as a cheap implement for cloth-working. Examples of tesserae made from sherds are known from Isleham and Burwell.

Tiles

Most varieties of Roman brick and tile have been found, among which the most common are roof-tiles, whose presence implies a fairly substantial building if only because of their weight. They were probably produced locally, probably from kilns near pottery-producing centres, such as those in Essex,[56] while the fairly common shell-gritted wares were probably produced in the Nene Valley. The common fabric of *tegulae* is brick-red to orange in colour, often with a partly or wholly unoxidized core, and is found throughout the region. Among other fabrics a hard grey type is found at Willingham, another grey variety and cream and buff wares at Chronicle Hills, Whittlesford (TL 452476). Brown fabrics are found at Hall Farm, Trumpington, and a softer fabric at Willingham. The curved imbrices are less common and are generally in the standard *tegula* fabric, but at Limlow Hill, Litlington, are in a brown sandy fabric akin to the local pottery.[57] Few floor-tiles are recorded, although in some villas the hypocaust *pilae* were made from stacks of tiles. There are a few instances of bricks used for flooring, and as quoins and bonding courses in masonry walls, for example at the Reach villa.

Examples of box flue-tiles are in the standard form in the common *tegula* fabric. At Chronicle Hills, Whittlesford (TL 452476), a softer orange fabric is used with finer combing; a creamy fabric is found at New Farm, Madingley, and brown fabrics are also found. Most flue-tiles were scoured with a comb in simple geometric and curvilinear patterns to facilitate the keying of mortar. The variety of pattern may have been used as a producer's trademark.[58] The fragment of a stamp appears on a box-tile from Comberton villa. Although not as common as the standard ware, a shell-gritted fabric occurs quite widely; except for some dark examples most have a light-brown surface and a thick grey core. In that fabric imbrices, *tegulae*, and flue-tiles are all recorded, the last with the usual combing, from sites such as Chronicle Hills, Whittlesford.

Like pottery, tiles were used for secondary purposes, including spindle-whorls and tesserae. The latter occur at various villas, including Landwade, Reach, Isleham, and Litlington. A tile from Paddock Street Farm, between Isleham and Soham, bears an indecipherable graffito, while one from Comberton has a boot print, another from Litlington the familiar print of a dog's paw.[59]

Wood

Timber appears to have been the principal building material, perhaps as much as 90 per cent in local buildings. The wooded claylands, especially the oak forests, were accessible and timber could have been conveyed, for the short distances involved, by road and water even to more remote districts of the treeless fenlands. In the fens transport by water from more distant woodlands to the west was available. Apart from

[55] Walker, in *Proc. C.A.S.* xv. 192–6.
[56] V.C.H. *Essex*, iii. 17.
[57] Clark, in *Proc. C.A.S.* xxxviii (1939), 170–6.

[58] As roller-stamped patterns were apparently a trade mark of kilns at Ashtead (Surr.).
[59] C.A.S. *Rep.* 14, p. 14.

buildings timber was used widely for many purposes, farm carts, household and farm utensils, and boats, not to mention coffins and grave-markers. The very scarcity of surviving remains in timber stands in sharp contrast with the presumed reality of Roman times. Besides the wooden coffins, a wooden spike has come from Arbury Road, and a wooden pin with chipped facets on the head from Horseheath.[60]

Textiles

Clothing was probably produced throughout the region for immediate local needs, by women, for whom the raw materials are unlikely to have been obtained from further afield than the local estate or market, except for the rare exotic fabrics such as silk. Local cloth-working is well attested by numbers of spindle-whorls (bone, pottery, and tile), loom-weights, bone spindles, and shuttles. The raw materials may have been produced in the fenlands and from the East Anglian Brecklands, where the woollen industry is indicated by the iron combs from Icklingham and Worlington (both Suff.).[61] Among the few surviving scraps of textile, a child burial, possibly of the late 2nd century, from Guilden Morden contained a fragment of cloth attached to a coin placed in the mouth of the deceased.[62] Elsewhere what appears to have been the funeral shroud of an old lady was found in a lead-lined stone coffin at Arbury Road, from which one fragment has a fine, plain weave, the other a coarse, matt weave.[63]

Leather

The leather sandals from White Mill Drain, Elm (TF 456011), are the only notable survival of an important material. The local cattle economy produced much leather, although whether or not most of it was removed from the area on the hoof remains unresolved.[64]

Bone

Easily procured and easily worked, bone was probably obtained locally throughout the region. The known sites of bone-working, at Grandford, March (TL 393996), the Roman settlement at the north end of the Bran Ditch, and the site of the Saxon cemetery at Burwell, were probably serving local needs only. They may have served the needs of a large estate, as at March, and some items may have been mass-produced for local sale.[65] Pins are by far the commonest object made of bone, and may be assigned to one of two classes, those with simple geometrically shaped heads and those with ornamental heads, and both are found throughout the region. The techniques of manufacturing the heads involved knife-carving and whittling, and lathe-turning. The Roman *acus* denoted a sewing needle, a pin for parting the hair, applying eyebrow paint, or dress-fastening, a surgical needle, the tongue of a brooch, and the needle for

[60] Fell, in *Proc. C.A.S.* xlix. 13–26 (Arbury Road); Catherine E. Parsons, ibid. xxxi (1931), 102 (Horseheath).

[61] J. P. Wild, *Textile Manufacture in Northern Roman Provinces* (1970), 9. Rather than Venta Belgarum (Winchester) the state weaving mill recorded as Venta in the late Roman *Notitia Dignitatum* (*Occidentalis*, xi. 60, ed. Seeck, p. 151) may be identified with Venta Icenorum; cf. *Roman Fenland*, 84 n. 115.

[62] The fibres are believed to be of vegetable origin: Wild, *Textile Manufacture*, 92.

[63] Fell, in *Proc. C.A.S.* xlix. 19. The origin remains uncertain, one analysis suggesting an indeterminate animal fibre, but a second and fuller a vegetable origin.

[64] *Roman Fenland*, p. 321.

[65] *Roman Fenland*, 197 (March); Fox and Palmer, in *Proc. C.A.S.* xxvii (1926), 21 (Bran Ditch); Lethbridge, in *Proc. C.A.S.* xxx (1929), 87–109 (Burwell). Other examples of bone-working occur from a roddon at Stuntney (Camb. Mus.), where a sheep tibia was found with four transverse knife cuts at the proximal end. From the filling above a grain-pit at War Ditches, Cherry Hinton, a long thin bone had been split and showed traces of slithers having been worked away at the edges. The filling of a well in Cambridge contained some bone pin-shafts in different stages of production: *Britannia*, vii (1976), 341.

trimming lamp-wicks. The decorated type seems generally to have been used for coiffure, while the plain forms were perhaps mainly dress-fasteners.[66]

It may be significant that many decorative motifs are common to bronze and bone pins. The former are much scarcer, and bone pins were perhaps cheaper substitutes, whose loss might be accepted with more equanimity. The occurrence of bone and other hairpins may reflect an elaborate attention to coiffure, perhaps following fashion depicted by imperial ladies on the Roman coinage of the 1st, 2nd, and early 3rd centuries. Their prevalence in the Roman period, compared with their absence in the pre-Roman era, is perhaps a telling pointer to a form of Roman cultural influence that otherwise would be almost impossible to chart among the peasant population of southeast Britain.

Among other bone objects are needles varying according to their function. Some were designed for working textiles or leather, while bone spindles are also found, and bone skewers and a possible shuttle have been found at War Ditches, Cherry Hinton.[67] Bone objects found in an inhumation burial at Guilden Morden include two bone armlets, almost identical (max. diam. c. 7·4 cm.), made of two thin strips of bone with bevelled section, curved around and secured with small iron rivets, and a comb nearly 12 cm. long with triangular terminals, on either face two handle-strips, secured by iron rivets, with chamfered edges and one with a simple incised line design.[68] The common bone counter is exemplified by a circular disc (diam. 2 cm.) with a flat outer rim from the Car Dyke. Most of the centre is slightly depressed and there is a drilled hole surrounded by a slightly raised rim.[69] Among other bone objects are fragments of inlay from the upper silting of the Iron Age enclosure ditch of Arbury Camp.[70]

The use of antlers from red deer is reflected by fragments of the proximal end of a tine found in mounds near Chippenham Fen, which may be of Roman date. The base of an antler, apparently shaped as a knife-handle, from Grunty Fen, Wilburton, is possibly Roman.[71]

Iron

The distinction between those iron implements made locally and those obtained from more distant workshops probably coincided with the degree of specialized function that they were intended to serve. The hoard of implements at Great Chesterford indicates perhaps a manufacturing centre, for which iron ore was obtained from deposits further afield, such as those in the Weald of Kent and Sussex or the Nene Valley which were extensively worked in the Roman period. Iron-working has been detected at Flaggrass, March (TL 434985), and iron slag at the Arbury Road estate and at Wendy (TL 3348) near the crossing of the Rhee by Ermine Street (1st to 4th century A.D.). Iron furnaces for local production, of a type known at Ashwicken (Norf.)

[66] Cf. illus. in *Jnl. Brit. Arch. Assoc.* [1st ser.], iv. 47. Use as dress-fasteners is discussed by Liversidge, *Britain in the Roman Empire*, 148. Some pins at Lydney (Glos.) were described by R. E. M. Wheeler as votive offerings: R. E. M. and T. V. Wheeler, *Excavations of . . . Site in Lydney Park* (1932), 41–2.

[67] One variety of needle is illustrated by a find from Arbury Road: Frend, in *Proc. C.A.S.* xlviii. 25 and plate IV (23). This has an increase in width continuous from the point to the finger end, the latter having a long and thin rectangular form with a round top and an eye. Examples of spindles from the basilican building at Ickleton have points at both ends with thickenings in the centre. For material from War Ditches see Hughes, in *Proc. C.A.S.* x. 452–81.

[68] Camb. Mus. Z 11459B. A similar comb was found at

Arbury Road: Frend, in *Proc. C.A.S.* xlviii (1955), 20 and plate IV. Such combs were probably for personal use, although one from the basilican building at Ickleton, which has a trapezoid form with a single edge, was for preparing wool or other textiles.

[69] Clark, in *Antiq. Jnl.* xxix. 145–63.

[70] Alexander, Excavation Rep. 1970. Among unidentified bone objects one found in 1911 at Horningsea is at least 7 cm. long and 1·1 cm. wide, a flattish piece of bone with slightly bevelled section whose vertical edges were made by detaching slithers with a knife, with a hole drilled at one end. Another enigmatic object, from Chaucer Road, Cambridge, has a surviving length of over 13 cm. The main shaft is round in section and tapered, while the head is spatulate and pierced for suspension.

[71] Camb. Mus.

and Sacrewell villa (Northants.), may have been working in the area during the Roman period.[72]

In contrast with bronze, more expensive and used only for specialized purposes, iron was the metal for everyday objects, of which by far the most common is the ubiquitous nail in a variety of sizes, all with the distinctive Roman characteristics of square section and flat head. Among iron knives from a number of sites, one from War Ditches, Cherry Hinton, has a straight continuous back, a handle tang, and a roughly right-angled triangular blade, another with shouldered back and elongated triangular blade was found in a pit beneath the skull of a calf at Milton gravel-pits (TL 482623).[73] Of the familiar varieties of iron keys, one from Reach villa has an E-shaped terminal and another from Ickleton has an elaborate bronze handle.[74] Iron brooches appear to have been a legacy of pre-Roman times, and the few examples known are not dated later than c. A.D. 55, including one associated with a bronze bow-and-fantail brooch in an inhumation at Guilden Morden.[75] There does not appear clear evidence for assigning a Roman date to the pair of iron compasses found in the 'Hunnybun's Ditch' in Cambridge, which is of late Saxon date, and a similar uncertainty must surround a find of chains, one with an attached hook, from Watts Fen Farm, Over (TL 379721), which may have been used for suspending a kettle.[76]

Excavation reports contain numerous references to 'fragments of unidentified iron objects', and even the Roman date remains unprovable for numerous surface finds. The horseshoes from West Fen, Willingham, fall into the latter category. Among other identified iron objects worthy of note are hippo-sandals from the ford at Arrington bridge and from Wendy, along with an ox-goad.[77] A manacle from Flat Bridge Road, Willingham, matches closely an example from London (Walbrook).[78] A pair of scissors or shears is known from Upper Delphs, Haddenham, a ballista bolt from Church End, Cottenham. Iron rings are known from West Fen north-east, Willingham, and from Horningsea and, in what seems a penannular variety, from Chronicle Hills, Whittlesford (TL 452476), and an iron pin with an open circular head from War Ditches, Cherry Hinton.[79] Two iron hooks, from the Whittlesford area (TL 454472) and Chronicle Hills (TL 452476), may be either reaping or bill-hooks, and from the latter site there is an iron spike with a rectangular head.[80]

Bronze

A fine bronze skillet found near Prickwillow (approx. TL 5982) has a handle decorated with mythical beasts and a winged genius in relief near the attachment end, and at the termination two dolphins also in relief. In between, the central part is decorated in niello with a scroll pattern and is stamped BODVOGENVS F(ECIT).[81] The three imported bronze jugs from Hauxton probably come from a disturbed burial.

[72] *Roman Fenland*, 221 (Flaggrass); Frend, in *Proc. C.A.S.* lii (1959), 25–7 (Arbury Road); *Britannia*, v (1974), 438 (Wendy). The 'blooms' from lumps of iron-stone from Abington Pigotts, assigned to the Early Iron Age, may from the evidence of the detailed report date to the Roman period: Fox, in *Proc. Prehist. Soc. E. Angl.* iv. 214.

[73] White, in *Proc. C.A.S.* lvi–lvii. 17 (War Ditches); *Roman Fenland*, 200 (Milton). Another shouldered knife is known from Cambridge (Shire Hall site), and an un-shouldered example with elongated triangular blade which may be Roman is a surface find from Crows Parlour, Thriplow (TL 454463).

[74] Camb. Mus.

[75] D. MacKreth, *Brooches* (1973), 12; Lethbridge, in *Proc. C.A.S.* xxxvi. 117; Camb. Mus. 37. 65 (Guilden Morden).

[76] *Roman Fenland*, 191; cf. Babington, *Ancient Cambs.*, pp. 82–3. The function of a fixture in the form of a bull from the northern Arbury Road site (TL 453613) remains uncertain.

[77] See Plate XIc. Lethbridge, in *Proc. C.A.S.* xlv. 61–2 (Arrington bridge); *Britannia*, v (1974), 438 (Wendy).

[78] *B.M. Roman Britain Guide* (1958), 53.

[79] Camb. Mus. (unpublished find from White's excavations).

[80] All surface finds. From the same area (TL 456468) was found an iron binding, and from Crows Parlour, Thriplow (TL 454463), an iron casing which fitted over a wood spike. The iron casing from Carter's Well, Grantchester, may have belonged to a ploughshare.

[81] See Plate XIIc. *Roman Fenland*, 229; *B.M. Roman Britain Guide* (1958), 38 and plate XVIII. Perhaps made in a continental workshop.

Parallels from Belgium suggest that they may have come from barrow burials of the wealthy, of which one, perhaps of settlers from the Continent, may have existed at Hauxton. One jug has a trefoil mouth, with a separately cast handle with a terminal in the form of a female mask. Another has a handle-terminal of birds' heads at the mouth and a bearded male, perhaps Pan or a satyr, on the body. The handle of the third terminates at the mouth in what are probably birds' heads and on the body in a pair of human feet. The vessels are dated to the 2nd or 3rd century.[82]

A group of bronze vessels was found stacked at Burwell comprising eight bowls of the 'Irchester type', three carinated cauldrons, one carinated bowl, a skillet, two penannular rings with incised decoration, and two unidentified vessels. The date of the deposit appears to be late-4th-century, and may signify the continuation of a native bronze industry into the Anglo-Saxon period, since vessels of similar type have been dated from the 3rd century to the 6th.[83] Other examples of bronze vessels include a handle from Fordham, paterae from Horningsea, and a 'ladle' from Shudy Camps.[84]

Most bronze brooch-types belong to the 1st and 2nd centuries. Several of the fairly common bow brooches, a class labelled 'Colchester derivatives', are known from Barrington, Burwell Fen, Cambridge, and Hauxton. A fine example of the 'thistle brooch' comes from Haslingfield, with a projecting 'flower' with bronze petals and centre cup filled with red enamel at the centre of its boss.[85] A bow-and-fantail brooch, the fan decorated in green enamel with a volute motif and red enamel, comes from the inhumation burial at Guilden Morden, which contained the iron brooch noted above.[86] In the Conybeare collection from Barrington there is a circular brooch with a setting of polychrome glass (blue, white, green, red, and yellow), and a circular bronze-gilt brooch with a glass intaglio of a beaked bird, probably an eagle.[87] A disc-brooch from Grantchester has at its centre a pentagonal scalloped motif filled with yellow and red enamel, and a rectangular plate-brooch from Cambridge is ornamented with four panels of red enamel while from either side protrudes the modelled head of a tortoise.[88] An unusually elaborate plate-brooch from Coton has an arch with a panel of blue enamel on an inverted triangle filled with blue enamel and with bulbous terminations filled with orange enamel. Most penannular brooches belong to the late Roman period, although some are earlier. A fine late example with knob terminals comes from Clayhithe, Horningsea (TL 501643), while another type of the same group is illustrated from New Fordey Farm, Soham, with flattened and curved-over terminals. Another late type is the crossbow, with a good example in gilt bronze with knob terminals from Barrington.[89] Although the recorded total is small the variety in type and quality of brooches indicates the prevalence of Roman dress fashions in different levels of society for most of the Roman period.

[82] See Plate XB. Liversidge, in *Proc. C.A.S.* li (1958), 8–11. For the female mask compare A. de Loë, in *Belgique Ancienne*, iii (1937), 91 fig. 26. For the date, *Archéologie*, 1954 (1), 181 plate 1; Den Boersterd, *Bronze Vessels in the Rijksmuseum G.M. Kam Nijmegen* (1956), 288–90.

[83] See Plate XA. A. Gregory, in *Proc. C.A.S.* lxvi (1977), 63–79. The fluted hemispherical bowl with zones of horizontal stamped decoration on the body and a stamped rim is of particular interest.

[84] *Proc. C.A.S.* xi (1907), 207 (Fordham); C.A.S. *Rep.* 45, p. xxxii (Horningsea); Babington, *Ancient Cambs.* (1883), 34 (Shudy Camps). A local origin is also assigned to some vessels of uncertain provenance, including a jug in the Banks collection, with the lower termination of the handle a mask flanked by dolphins. A bowl-cum-ladle with an elaborate handle in the Cole Ambrose collection is labelled as coming from Stuntney near Ely. The handle

terminates at the rear in a mask, with a front projection in the form of an animal head, and is attached to the body at the flanks with palmettes. Fragments of a large thin vessel are known from Horningsea.

[85] MacKreth, *Brooches*, 16; R. G. Collingwood and I. A. Richmond, *Arch. of Roman Britain*, 293 no. 91 (thistle-brooch based on Collingwood Group W).

[86] Lethbridge, in *Proc. C.A.S.* xxxvi. 117; Camb. Mus. 37. 65; cf. Collingwood and Richmond, *Arch. of Roman Britain*, 294 no. 96 (Group X).

[87] Henig, *Roman Gemstones*, ii, p. 105 no. 824.

[88] Illustrated by Liversidge, *Britain in the Roman Empire*, 145, fig. 58c.

[89] *Roman Fenland*, 224; cf. Lethbridge and O'Reilly, in *Proc. C.A.S.* xxxiii. 166 (Clayhithe); from Barrington, Camb. Mus. acc. Z 15992.

Among several bronze pins, a late Roman spiral-headed type was found in a field near Comberton; an ibex-headed pin at Newnham; a bronze pin with a flat triangular head ornamented with ring and dot motif at Cambridge. From the site at Upper Delphs, Haddenham, has come a horizontally fluted handle with a 'door-knob' termination, a pin with simple ovoid head, and an object over 30 cm. with a long thin shaft, a broken end splayed and flattened, and a knob-like head ornamented with radiating grooves. A bronze needle was found at an unspecified location near Cambridge.[90] Of two bronze bracelets from an inhumation burial at Guilden Morden, one consisted of a plaited strip of flat wire with hook terminals, while the other was a narrow untwisted strip, flat inside but slightly bevelled outside. From a cremation in the same cemetery comes a bracelet in twisted bronze wire.[91] Other bronze objects include rings from various places and some wire from Cambridge. A simple finger-ring from Newnham has a terminal in the form of a key, and a bronze finger-ring is known from West Fen, Willingham (TL 395718). Small simple keys with ring handles are known from Comberton, Barnwell, Foxton, and Orwell. Finds of bronze styli attest the spread of literacy. One from Newnham has a globular termination with small knob attachments at one end, pointed at the other, and another from Cambridge has a fine wedge at one end and a point at the other. Bronze styli are also recorded from Anglo-Saxon burials at Linton Heath. A 4th-century bronze seal from the Arbury Road excavation is heart-shaped, and one from Croydon circular with a diamond and dot motif in red enamel on a green ground on the lid.[92]

Bronze was used in objects of other material. A wooden casket in the Girton cremation had six rings and eight bronze bosses in the form of boars' heads attached to the wood with an iron pin. The bronze handle of an iron knife from Croxton has the form of a hound chasing a hare, rendered in a style reminiscent of the Hunt cup. Among less common objects what was the bronze sheath of perhaps a wooden rod and sceptre, with a phallic bronze pendant, was found among a hoard of iron objects in a hole in the side of a grave at Guilden Morden. It may have belonged to the instruments of a religious official. A child burial in the same cemetery contained a bell which may have been worn on a shoe, and a bell and another object of uncertain purpose were found at Upper Delphs, Haddenham (TL 409737). A bronze spoon from Horningsea has simple decoration on the handle at the bowl end, a marked shoulder, and an oval bowl. Another from the Stacks east, Willingham (TL 421707), is of beaten bronze with a tanged shoulder and simple ovoid bowl. A rare object is the rectangular mirror in white bronze from Malton, Orwell. A bronze locket from Cherry Hinton has flat covers decorated with a cruciform design incised in dotted lines. In more utilitarian fields the probable horse-harness mount from Haslingfield (TL 417527), an open-work disc with Celtic triquetra within a circle, is either pre-Roman or early Roman. From the Roman town of Cambridge comes a bronze terret.[93]

Bronze Sculpture

The remarkable bronze bust from Bullock's Haste, Cottenham (TL 46557038), representing either the emperor Marcus Aurelius (161–80) or more probably his son

---

[90] Walker, in *Proc. C.A.S.* xiv. 239–41; K. Pretty, in A. C. C. Brodribb *et al.*, *Excavations at Shakenoak*, pt. iii (priv. print. 1972), 85.

[91] Guilden Morden cremation no. 2 in 1937 excavation.

[92] Frend, in *Proc. C.A.S.* xlviii. 25 (Arbury Road); Neville, in *Arch. Jnl.* xi. 96. Several Roman objects have come to light in Anglo-Saxon burial grounds.

[93] *Roman Fenland*, 206, 208 (Upper Delphs and the Stacks); *Proc. C.A.S.* xxi (1919), 106 (Cherry Hinton); Fox and Lethbridge, ibid. xxvii. 58 fig. 6 (Guilden Morden sheath); Lethbridge, ibid. xlv (1952), 65–6 (Haslingfield); Camb. Mus. 63. 701 (terret); Lethbridge, in *Proc. C.A.S.* xxxvi. 109–20 (Guilden Morden child burial). A bronze object from Cambridge or the locality has been identified as an ear-spoon or similar toilet instrument: Camb. Mus.

Commodus (180–192), comes from a shrine perhaps associated in some way with the imperial cult. The hollowed bust was attached to a body or perhaps a wall-bracket. The features are of a bearded and moustached emperor, with the hair indicated as modelled curls by incised lines. The Corinthian helmet has the form of a human head with oriental features, with hair portrayed by a series of pecked lines. On the forehead of the helmet there is an oval penannular design, and on the sides of the head above the ears are other designs in the form of a flattened S. On the bust itself the drapery is represented conventionally with a gathering clasp at the right shoulder, and three snakes on an aegis appear as wavy ridges. One snake comes from the right shoulder, and one from the left, the two meeting just below the lower end of the sternum. The third comes from the left side of the neck and terminates towards the inner edge of the left pectoral. The bust has been described as 'a blend of Celtic and classical Roman elements'.[94] There may have been another shrine at the Hempsals, Willingham (TL 436706), whence has come a small bronze bust (10 cm. high) of the emperor Antoninus Pius (A.D. 138–61). The bust, which is partially broken in front and pierced with a round hole behind, is recessed to receive some baton-like object. The narrow face, short curly beard, and thick growth of hair low on the centre of the brow, all suggest that it represents the emperor Pius. On the crown and back the locks of hair are rendered carefully in low relief, although the crude representation of the features, notably the slanting and somewhat staring eyes, are held to represent the work of a provincial craftsman.[95] The two busts suggest that a number of small shrines, some associated with particular emperors, were established throughout the fenlands, particularly if, as has been suggested, the area formed an imperial estate.

The statuette of Hercules from Sutton, Ely (approx. TL 4478), represents the young hero standing naked, with an upraised right hand which once held his club, while the left holds a cloak, and he wears the skin of the Nemean lion as a head-dress.[96] The same hero appears in a miniature statuette from the Ely district (TL 5480) as older and bearded, standing naked with the skin of the lion draped over his left fore-arm. His club rests in his left hand against the upper arm, with the right arm stretched out downwards. The same district has yielded a second statuette with similar attributes.[97]

The statuette of Mercury from Manea Fen (approx. TL 4990) represents the god standing naked, the weight of his relaxed body on his stiffened right leg, while the left is slightly bent at the knee. A short drape is arranged over the left shoulder, curled behind the back of the upper left arm and over the left fore-arm; the left hand probably held the herald's staff (*caduceus*), while the right is outstretched and holds an object which may be a purse. Small wings protrude from the temples and a garland on the head is secured by a ribbon tied at the neck, with single strands brought forward to each shoulder. Another statuette of the same deity is reported from Cambridge (Castle Hill) but appears to be no longer extant.[98]

Two statuettes of Venus are known from Ely (approx. TL 5480). One (now in Cambridge Museum) represents a tall and thin young woman naked and is executed in a very provincial style, the anatomical features, especially the face, represented superficially. The breasts are small and the left hand covers the pubic region, while the right hangs down the side slightly forward. The fillet binding the front of the hair is represented with simple incised decoration. A statuette of Diana from Bassingbourn

[94] See frontispiece; Toynbee, *Art in Roman Britain*, 125 no. 5; cf. *Roman Fenland*, 212; below, pp. 84–5, for other examples of bronze sculpture.

[95] See Plate XIVG. *J.R.S.* xxxix (1949), 19, plate 2; cf. Toynbee, *Art in Roman Britain*, 124 no. 3 and plate 3.

[96] See Plate XIA. F. M. Heichelheim, in *Proc. C.A.S.* xxxvii (1937), 52; cf. *Roman Fenland*, 215.

[97] See Plate XIA. *Roman Fenland*, 229; cf. Heichelheim, in *Proc. C.A.S.* xxxvii. 52–3 and plate IIIB.

[98] *Roman Fenland*, 220; cf. Heichelheim, in *Proc. C.A.S.* xxxvii. 52 (Manea Fen); Downing Coll., Bowtell MSS. ii. 191 (Cambridge).

represents a rather podgy figure in most uninspired fashion. She wears the short flared skirt and a short-sleeved mantle folded double. The right arm is bent at the elbow holding in the hand an object which has been lost. The hair was gathered to the crown of the forehead and secured by a fillet.[99]

The small bronze head of a male Celtic deity[1] from the Girton College settlement has a socket on the back for attaching it by pin to a body or some fixture, while the unfinished appearance of the back suggests that it was intended for a niche where only the front and sides would be visible. The portrayal of the face may be described as 'provincial' rather than 'classical', with the features crudely executed. The eyes are lozenge-shaped raised rims, the mouth small and poorly indicated. Two projecting knobs on the lower chin represent a beard, and some form of tiara appears on the forehead. Another miniature statuette from Ely (approx. TL 5480) represents a genius, walking, wearing a double-folded mantle, and with shoulder-length hair; the left hand carries a torch which rests on the shoulder, and the right holds a flagon down by the side.[2]

No generalization is supportable on the evidence of these bronze sculptures; none of them appears to have been made locally and some may be imports from the Continent. The concentration in the fenland and fen edge may be wholly accidental.

Lead and Silver

Neither lead nor silver appears to have been used widely in the region. A silver finger-ring with snake's head terminals was found at Ditton (probably Fen Ditton), and another ring is recorded from the Gog Magog Hills.[3]

The lead linings of the Arbury Road coffins originate from two different sources, since only that of the female burial contains tin. Lead pipes are known in the Comberton villa, a large lead vat was found at the Stacks north, Willingham (TL 421709), and other lead objects come from Horningsea, Gorefield in Leverington (TF 417120), Reach villa, where a piece of lead contains an iron bolt, and Whittlesford (TL 4535 4735). Lead tanks supposedly used in Christian baptism are known from Icklingham (Suff.), the Ouse near Huntingdon, Willingham, and near Cambridge.[4]

Pewter

Pewter manufacture in Britain began during the 3rd century, when workshops in Somerset are found using Mendip lead. Since, however, most pewter finds are from eastern Britain there may have been other workshops in that area. Socially the use of pewter might indicate a class below that which could have silver on the table. Numerous pewter finds in Cambridgeshire and adjacent areas begin with a flanged bowl from Arbury Road in a building demolished perhaps in the 3rd century.[5]

[99] See Plate XIA. *Roman Fenland*, 229; cf. Heichelheim, in *Proc. C.A.S.* xxxvii. 61 and plate IIIE.

[1] See Plate VIID.

[2] See Plate XIA. *Roman Fenland*, 229. A fragment from the head of a small figurine in native style was found in surface collections at Haslingfield across the river from Cantelupe Farm (TL 432539). Among some lesser items, there is a bronze statuette (nature unspecified) from Parson Drove (approx. TF 370080): cf. *Roman Fenland*, 298; Fowler, in *Proc. C.A.S.* xliii. 17. The bronze bust of a satyr is reported from Linton: Camden, *Brit.* (1806), ii. 227; cf. Babington, *Ancient Cambs.* 35. A bronze horse with what is perhaps a pricket rising from its back was found, associated with a coin of Pertinax (A.D. 193), in Malcolm Street, Cambridge: C.A.S. *Rep.* 14, p. 13; cf. W. H. Rosser, in *Archaeologia*, xxviii (1840), 441–3.

[3] Neville, in *Arch. Jnl.* xi. 213 n. The Ditton ring is illustrated in Liversidge, *Britain in the Roman Empire*, 143 fig. 56b.

[4] Fell, in *Proc. C.A.S.* xlix. 13–23 (Arbury Road); Babington, *Ancient Cambs.* 23 (Comberton); *Roman Fenland*, 208 (Willingham), 324 (Gorfield); Liversidge, in *Camb. Region, 1965*, ed. J. A. Steers, 130 (baptismal tanks).

[5] Peal, in *Proc. C.A.S.* lx (1967), 19–37; Alexander, Excavation Rep. 1967, 13. Pointing to a coincidence of distribution between hoards of pewter, bronze bowls, ironwork, and late coins, especially in Cambs. and W. Norf., W. H. Manning has suggested that the area may have been in the 'front line' of barbarian incursion. He suggests also that the iron hoards may be votive and connected with a 'resurgence of pagan cults' in late Roman times, and dates the deposition of the Great Chesterford hoard to the late 4th or early 5th cent.: *Britannia*, iii (1972), 248; cf. ibid. 236.

A remarkable flanged pewter tazza with Christian symbols[6] may have come from Sutton. The pewter from an extinct river course in Isleham Fen included two jugs, three bowls, two tazze, one dish, a pedestalled bowl, and many indented beakers, all of which may have been part of a cargo either lost or thrown overboard. One of the jugs, less elegant than other local finds, has a neck reduced to a simple *torus* moulding, with a curvilinear handle, instead of a fluted cylinder, with its termination at the body a conventionalized ivy-leaf plate.[7] A fine jug from Roll's Lode, near Quanea Hill, Ely (TL 573792), has a flared rim and a flange half-way up its tall neck, while below the elegant curving body is a simple outflaring base. Grooves on the body and the neck were applied on a lathe. The upright handle is a horizontally fluted tapering cylinder.[8] Another jug comes from the Broads, Burwell (approx. TL 5969), where a dish was also found; the jug is similar to the Quanea jug but less elegant.[9] There is a pewter jug among a hoard from the bed of the Landwade stream (approx. TL 6267), while another hoard is believed to have been found at Tiled House Farm, Stretham (TL 523732), associated with glass vessels and numerous large coloured beads.[10] Among other finds there is pewter in the British Museum designated 'Coldham', three dishes found together at the Poplars, Manea (TL 478898), a pewter bowl from Stonea, Wimblington, six platters and a bowl from Sutton, and a pewter plate probably from near Finch's Farm, Stuntney, Ely. Parts of three plates are known from Horningsea, and there is a tazza from Pout Hall, Burwell, at the junction of Burwell and Reach lodes.[11]

Glass

Although some clinker and burnt glass was found in the Horseheath excavations[12] it appears that most glass used was not manufactured locally. Intact glass vessels generally come from cemeteries. Many sites have produced fragments of glass vessels, notably Shingay, the Stacks south in Willingham, Castle Hill and Arbury Road in Cambridge, Wimpole, and War Ditches in Cherry Hinton.[13] Some fine vessels come from the Girton cremation, notably a cremation urn of green glass with a thick-sided hexagonal body, a short and narrow neck with a thick rolled flat lip and the right-angle strap handle attached below the lip and fluted at the shoulder. Such cremation bottles are common as cremation urns in Britain, and good examples are found at Wicken Fen. Although the basic shape seems to have persisted there are variations in size and proportion. There is a tall example from Haslingfield, and a large vessel in a grave group from Litlington, while from the Arbury Road area come a large round bottle or jar, a variant of the square type, two standard square bottles in clear glass, and a third in green glass.[14] Among other vessels in the Girton cremation there is a vase of clear,

[6] See Plates XIIA, XIIB.

[7] See Plate XIIIA. *Roman Fenland*, 237; Lethbridge and O'Reilly, in *Proc. C.A.S.* xxxiii. 165–6 and plate VI; Lethbridge, ibid. xxxiv. 93.

[8] See Plate XIIIA. *Roman Fenland*, 229; cf. Lethbridge and O'Reilly, in *Proc. C.A.S.* xxxiii. 165; Camb. Mus. 32. 224.

[9] See Plate XIIIA. *Proc. C.A.S.* xxxiii, plate V (dish); *Roman Fenland*, 225; cf. Camb. Mus. 1883. 771 (jug). The lower half of the jug body is a series of flat facets below an incised band of cable ornament mid-way on the body. Its lower border is a single line while the upper border consists of simple leftwards-inclined short lines between two lines.

[10] *Roman Fenland*, 235; cf. Lethbridge and O'Reilly, in *Proc. C.A.S.* xxxiii. 165 (Landwade); *Roman Fenland*, 226; cf. T. Mackay, *Reminiscences of Albert Pell* (1908), 103 (Stretham). It has been suggested that in cases of deliber-

ate hoarding the vessels might have been placed in chests and sunk in a stream, their position marked by small buoys: *Proc. C.A.S.* xxxiii. 166.

[11] *Roman Fenland*, 215 (Sutton), 216 (Manea), 219 (Stonea), 228 (Stuntney), 319 (B.M.); Camb. Mus. (Horningsea); cf. L. C. G. Clarke, in *Proc. C.A.S.* xxxi (1931), 66–75 (Sutton), 166 (Stuntney); Lethbridge and O'Reilly, ibid. xxxiii. 165–6 (Burwell); C. A. Peal, ibid. lx (1967), 30 (B.M.; Sutton); C.B.A. Group 7, *Bulletin* 2 (Manea).

[12] Parsons, in *Proc. C.A.S.* xxxi. 103; Camb. Mus.

[13] Camb. Mus. (Shingay); *Roman Fenland*, 209 (the Stacks south); Browne, in *Proc. C.A.S.* lxv (1) (Cambridge area).

[14] *Roman Fenland*, 227; cf. Camb. Mus. 19. 82–3 (Wicken Fen); Camb. Mus. acc. 1887. 8 (Haslingfield); Camb. Mus. (Litlington); Frend, in *Proc. C.A.S.* xlix (1956), 25 (Arbury Road).

blown glass with a short tapered cylindrical body, everted lip, and flattish base-plate. The so-called 'duck bowl' is probably an Egyptian import from Alexandria. Its form with a foot-ring base is reminiscent of a Dragendorf 18/31 samian vessel in a translucent glass with a slightly greenish tint. On the underneath a duck and Nilotic plants are incised. On the inside of the body base is a depressed ring and on the underside of the rim a series of closely spaced oval facets.[15]

A good-quality jug in pale blue glass from Litlington[16] has a wide squat body with ribs and a simple foot, a tall and narrow neck, and a right-angle strap handle with a Medusa medallion at the body junction. Originating probably from the Seine–Rhine region it dates perhaps to the early 2nd century. A vessel from the same site, with a base of tapering clear glass and yellow trailed decoration around the outside, also originates perhaps from the same continental district but at a later date, perhaps the late 2nd or early 3rd century. The same site has also produced the lower part of a jug in amber glass with brown ribs. Associated with a 4th-century red colour-coated bowl in a burial at Arbury Road was a jug in greenish glass with a double rim, strap handle and foot-ring base. Unguent bottles, with squat bulbous body, tall narrow neck, and flared lip, are common in burials, and an example comes along with the bronze bracelet from a cremation at Guilden Morden.[17] In a group from Hauxton mill, probably from a disturbed burial, was a colourless flask, a jug, and two bowls, dated to A.D. 150–250 and probably imports from the Rhineland. A squat medium-mouthed jar in clear glass with a very short neck and horizontal rim comes from Hatley Park, an area sparse in settlement.[18]

Window-glass was probably widely used, even in timber buildings, notably in Cambridge where as yet no substantial masonry structures have been found, besides villas and some of the 'lesser' settlements. Among glass beads, the Webb collection from Litlington includes a simple ring, two shaped as two inverted truncated pyramids placed end to end, and several pieces in blue glass fashioned as pentagonal cylinders. From Croydon have come two cylindrical beads in blue frit glass.[19]

RELIGION AND BURIAL

Religion

ASIDE from the widespread evidence for burial ritual discussed below, there is some specific evidence relating to religious observances in both Roman and native traditions. The remarkable hoard from the Hempsals, Willingham (TL 436706), still poses a number of unanswered questions. Among various objects packed in a wooden box were three fragments of one or more bronze sceptres or maces. One fragment has the form of a knobbed club similar to that normally associated with Hercules. A second object is a cylinder with four figures in high relief, a male deity, a wheel crowned with an eagle, a dolphin, and a three-horned bull's head. The third principal find is the bust of Anto-

---

[15] Liversidge, in *Proc. C.A.S.* li (1958), 12; cf. D. B. Harden, *Roman Glass from Karanis*, 66 fig. 1c.

[16] See Plate XVIA.

[17] Fox, *Arch. Camb. Region*, plate xxv (4) (Litlington); Camb. Mus. 52. 448 (Arbury Road), and no. 2 in 1937 excavations (Guilden Morden).

[18] Liversidge, in *Proc. C.A.S.* li (1958), 12–16 (Hauxton mill), with Rhineland origin suggested by D. B. Harden; Camb. Mus. 67. 235 (Hatley Park). Other vessels probably

from a burial are two from Barnwell, the first a beaker in clear glass with faceted body dated to the late 1st or early 2nd cent.: *B.M. Roman Britain Guide* (1966), plate 11(2) and p. 42; the other, a flagon in blue-green glass having a tall, narrow neck and a conical body with thin, diagonal ribbing, is also late-1st- or early-2nd-cent.: ibid. plate 12(11). See below, Plates VIIA, VIIc.

[19] Camb. Mus.

ninus Pius described above. The rest of the hoard consists of eight fragments of bronze tubes, perhaps part of maces, two miniature horsemen in bronze, the upper part of a helmeted figure in bronze, an owl and an eagle in bronze, a face-mask with two projecting loops, two jet beads, an amber ring, three glass beads, a single-link bit, a bronze mask, a bust with fillet or veil, a boar's head with a single horn, and a lion's head attached to a rectangular plate.[1]

In the view of M. Rostovtzeff, who identified the bust as of Commodus, the male deity on the cylinder was the Celtic lord of heaven, earth, and water, and the three large fragments belonged to a mace forming part of the 'official insignia of a magistrate of some neighbouring municipality', kept normally in a public building or consecrated in a temple, of either Celtic gods or the imperial cult. He linked the mace with a Hercules–Commodus cult, which may have become widespread after the victories of Ulpius Marcellus in northern Britain in A.D. 184.[2] Against this A. Alföldi rejected the association of the imperial bust, which he identifies with Antoninus Pius (138–61) rather than Commodus, with the remains of the 'mace', and asserted that the representation of the club is not an indication of the Commodus–Hercules cult and if it had been joined with the bust could not have been a sceptre since the head of the emperor would have been held upside down. Moreover he concluded that the dimensions of the two pieces preclude their having been joined together. Alföldi suggested that the club was a votive offering in a shrine probably associated with Diana, while the tubular fragments and the imperial bust came from a sceptre.[3] Among the Celtic associations of the hoard the male deity on the cylinder is Taranis, the Celtic Jupiter, who holds a thunderbolt and tramples a victim underfoot, and is accompanied by an eagle on a wheel, an unusual combination of symbols from Celtic iconography. The three-horned bull represents the horned fertility god, an important Celtic deity particularly associated with Gaul, where the piece may have been made. The dolphin on the cylinder has associations with wells and springs, exemplified at the Carrawburgh Coventina shrine on Hadrian's Wall, and is likely to have been venerated throughout the fenlands. The bronze horsemen represent either gods or models of cavalry, the owl is one of two from Roman Britain not in the familiar role of Minerva's bird, and the single-horned boar's head may have been a ritual implement for prognostication.[4] Those and other bronze figurines described earlier seem to attest the presence of shrines in the fenlands and parallels have been drawn with parts of Belgium and the Rhineland, which may even support the notion of settlers originating from those areas.[5] Among evidence of possible shrines, it has been suggested that a temple to Taranis stood near St. Peter's church, Cambridge, although the evidence seems far from conclusive. The remains of a temple or mausoleum are reported from Cotton's Drove, Elm (TL 497039), although the date is uncertain, and the discovery of an altar with an associated structure in the same locality may denote the existence of a temple.[6]

The sculptured panel depicting an armed figure from the Arbury Road site may indicate some religious usage for a building.[7] At Mutlow Hill, Great Wilbraham, during the

---

[1] See Plate XIV. *Roman Fenland*, 209–10, with full references.

[2] Rostovtzeff, in *J.R.S.* xiii. 91 sqq.

[3] *J.R.S.* xxxix. 19 sqq. The identification with Antoninus Pius is accepted by Toynbee, *Art in Roman Britain*, 124 no. 3.

[4] Discussed by Anne Ross, *Pagan Celtic Britain* (1967), 275–6 (Taranis), 129, 303–4 (fertility god), 49, 351 (sceptre), 199 (cavalrymen), 274 (owl), 311 and plate 80a (boar's head).

[5] Heichelheim, in *Proc. C.A.S.* xxxvii. 52–67; cf.

Applebaum, in *Ag.H.R.* vi (1958), 80.

[6] Heichelheim, in *Proc. C.A.S.* xxxvii. 55; cf. Pauly-Wissowa, *Realencyclopädie*, s.v. 'Tierdamonen', col. 935–6 (Cambridge); *Roman Fenland*, 322, 324 (Elm).

[7] Discovered in building I, site II (period IIa); Alexander, Excavation Rep. 1967, 8–9; cf. *J.R.S.* lvii (1967), 189. Two parallel rows of pits dated to the 4th cent. were lined with hexagonal roof-tiles of Northants. limestone and filled with fine ash, broken bones of domestic animals, pottery, oyster shells, and nails, whose collective function remains uncertain.

excavation of a circular structure of chalk blocks, Roman brooches, bracelets, and coins dating from the 1st century to the 4th were found, and there was a clearly defined belt, c. 3·75 metres wide, of Roman pottery and objects deposited around the barrow, which have the appearance of votives around a shrine of great antiquity, perhaps venerated since Bronze Age times.[8] The discovery of pottery with applied decorative face-mouldings has been interpreted as evidence for crude rites among the lower classes, where the head and phallus had both funerary and fertility associations.[9]

The most notable evidence for Christian worship is a flanged pewter tazza which may have been part of the Sutton hoard; if it was, all the vessels in the hoard may have had liturgical functions perhaps as parts of a church collection. The flange decoration consists of an incised chi-rho monogram flanked by alpha and omega, adjacent to which are two peahens and a peacock. Opposite the monogram is an owl and alongside are four Nereids, perhaps symbols alluding to regeneration and baptism. The vessel, which has eight points to the flange, may have been a portable font and may be native work of the 4th century. The accompanying cursive inscription has not yet been satisfactorily interpreted, although one suggestion deduces that the tazza belonged to the furniture of a bishop and clergy.[10]

Burial

Cremation appears to have been the commonest burial rite throughout the 1st and 2nd centuries, and probably for most of the 3rd.[11] It is present in all areas, either in isolation or as part of a cemetery group ranging from two or three burials into hundreds. In some larger cemeteries, containing hundreds of cremations and inhumations, the former are generally earlier, although there are exceptions, as at Litlington where inhumations have been found below cremations. Cremation, however, was already well established in pre-Roman times and some pre-Roman cemeteries continued in use during Roman times, for example at Guilden Morden where Belgic cremations in pots have been found.

In Cambridge the area of Gravel Hill appears to have contained a large number of cremations, both contained in and associated with pottery, belonging to the extramural cemetery north of the Roman town. Whereas little is known of that cemetery or of the large one at Dam Hill on the south side,[12] more is recorded about the remarkable cemetery at Litlington (TL 314420), presumably attached to the near-by villa, and occupying an area 35 by 25 metres enclosed by a wall of flint and brick. Rows of cremations are arranged east–west separated by one metre intervals. There is great variety in the individual burials, some in tile cists, others in wooden boxes or flint enclosures, while several were simply placed beneath the cover of a single tile. The common Roman grave-goods are typical at Litlington, with the jar containing the cremation accompanied by a pottery flagon and dish. Some cremation urns were covered with large dishes, several in samian ware. One such group of the late 2nd century was composed of samian forms (Dr. 33, 35, 18/31, and 36). Piles of wood ash in the south-east and south-west corners may be the rakings from funeral pyres. Precise association of some grave-goods cannot now be easily established, including a small

[8] Neville, in *Arch. Jnl.* ix. 226–9; Fox and Palmer, in *Proc. C.A.S.* xxiv (1923), 45, 48.

[9] Ross, *Pagan Celtic Britain*, 104 n. 1 and fig. 8. For a pottery vessel with a neck-mask from Cambridge see Toynbee, *Art in Britain under the Romans*, 406 n. 2 and plate 21g, and above, Plate IXd.

[10] See Plates XIIa, XIIb. *Roman Fenland*, 215; cf. Clarke, in *Proc. C.A.S.* xxxi. 66–75; Toynbee, *Art in Roman Britain*, 176 no. 121.

[11] This section is not a comprehensive gazetteer but rather a survey of burials selected to illustrate the variety of burial rights. The entire section owes much to the work of Miss Joan Liversidge (in progress) on burials of the Cambridge region.

[12] Babington, in *Proc. C.A.S.* ii. 289–92.

pair of tongs, perhaps for gathering ashes, an incense shovel, and a 2nd-century incense-burner in white ware from the Rhineland with the name INDV(L)CIVS spelt out in perforations. Other grave-goods, though not all certainly from the cremations, include bronze bracelets, brooches, glass beads, a jet bangle, a cornelian bead, a bone pin and needle, and glass vessels.[13]

The cemetery at Guilden Morden (TL 285400) is somewhat better known through having been excavated more than once. Among the finds is a 3rd-century Rhenish beaker with VTERE FELIX applied *en barbotine*.[14] Cremation continued there well into the 3rd century and perhaps even into the 4th. Some cremations in pots have no accompanying goods, although most have other pots associated, often in samian ware as at Litlington. Other grave-goods included bronze armlets, and in one grave, where the cremation vessel was accompanied by other pots, were an iron lamp and the hobnails from a pair of boots buried with the deceased, a practice that appears to have been widespread at Guilden Morden.

A good example of a smaller cemetery where both inhumation and cremation were practised is that at Girton College (TL 425608), whose long history began in the 1st century and continued into the pagan Saxon period, a continuity which may be matched in the near-by settlement. Some monuments may have incorporated stone sculptures, whose fragments, notably of a lion and a human torso, were found along with tile fragments in rubbish pits. Among notable cremations in the cemetery, one in a grey flagon dates to the late 1st century, another was contained in a wooden chest and accompanied by an iron lamp and its hanger, a green glass bottle with handles, two Trajanic–Antonine samian dishes, and other pottery. The third was altogether more lavish, where the wooden chest contained the hexagonal glass cremation urn, along with which were a beaker in clear glass, a glass decanter, and a glass perfume bottle stamped on the base C. LVCRETI FESTIVI. An imported Egyptian glass bowl with incised designs of a duck on the base and Nilotic plants, a Gallic bowl in brown lead-glazed pottery, a samian dish and cup by Trajanic–Antonine potters, and a pottery flagon were also found. Eight bronze bosses in the form of boars' heads and other metal fittings may have come from the wooden chest or from another container buried with it.[15]

Many of the numerous individual cremation burials may in reality belong to much larger cemeteries still awaiting discovery. At Fulbourn a burial in 'a square brick grave', perhaps a tile burial, contained glass and pottery vessels. Near Cantelupe Farm, Haslingfield (TL 412529), a cremation was contained in a red globular amphora. At Arbury Road (TL 45126093) a cremation was placed in a samian Dragendorf form 37 bowl of Mercator (A.D. 145–70), while a little to the south (TL 45226049) a high-quality cremation contained four rectangular glass bottles, two of which contained bone, and a stack of samian vessels (two of form 35, three of form 36, one of form 46, and one of Curle form 15), together with an iron lamp and a pottery flagon. At Red Church Field, Linton (TL 571462), a cremation placed in a pit contained pottery of the early Roman period, a bronze brooch, and a bronze stud in the form of a lion's head. The stud may have come from a box, or from a collar of the dog whose bones

---

[13] See Plates IIIB, XIIIB. Kempe, in *Archaeologia*, xxvi. 368–76; C. Roach Smith, *Collectanea Ant.* i. 22 and plate 12; Fox, *Arch. Camb. Region*, 189 and plate xxi (3–3a).
[14] Fox and Lethbridge, in *Proc. C.A.S.* xxvii. 49–71; Lethbridge, ibid. xxxvi. 109–20; K. Jeffries, in *J.R.S.* lix (1969), 223; Lewis, in *Proc. C.A.S.* iv. 337–41. A lamp allegedly from Guilden Morden cemetery and of Egyptian origin, e.g. Walters, *Cat. of Gk. and Roman Lamps in B.M.*

(1914), no. 758 and plate xxv, is of doubtful authenticity and provenance: ex inf. Miss Joan Liversidge.
[15] See Plates XVB, XVIB, XVIc. Hollingworth and O'Reilly, *Cemetery at Girton Coll.* 32 sqq.; *Roman Fenland*, 198; Babington, *Ancient Cambs.* 37–40; *C.A.S. Rep.* 41, p. li; Fox, *Arch. Camb. Region*, 193; Toynbee, *Art in Roman Britain*, 185 no. 140.

were found along with the burial.[16] The quality of the two glasses in the cremation at Barnwell show that this burial practice was employed among the rich.[17]

A particular ritual associated with cremation burial is that of 'killing a pot', and such a practice is exemplified at Pound Ground, Willingham (TL 432716), where the base of a vessel has been deliberately perforated.[18] The cremation burials of the wealthy are distinguished by the quality of their grave-goods, often expensive imports, from the much larger number of humbler burials where the ashes of the dead were deposited in their own domestic pottery often with the upper parts broken off to allow the insertion of the contents.

The sporadic occurrence of the inhumation burial rite during the first two centuries of Roman rule continues a non-Belgic pre-Roman tradition. It became the dominant rite during the 3rd century and is almost universal in the 4th. At Guilden Morden one inhumation of the Iron Age or very early Roman period has a flagon in buff ware at the shoulder, a grey beaker by the left thigh, and at the left knee a *terra nigra* platter containing four mutton cutlets. Some inhumations at Limlow Hill, Litlington, may be as early as the 1st century, and near Cambridge at the sewage farm several early inhumations accompanied by pots are recorded. Similar burials of the 1st and 2nd centuries have been found at War Ditches, Cherry Hinton, including one skeleton accompanied by an imitation of a samian form in fine grey ware with decoration of incised dots and semi-circles, and another was accompanied by a 1st-century brooch.[19]

Like cremations, inhumation burials are found both in small groups and in large cemeteries throughout the whole area, although among large cemeteries the three at Dam Hill, Hauxton mill, and Limlow Hill and the extramural cemeteries of Cambridge are poorly known.[20] Little is recorded about the precise details of the 250 inhumations from Litlington, although more is known of the burials from Guilden Morden, where several variations in the burial rite are found, with the burials orientated in all directions. Many had no grave goods, some were contained in wooden coffins indicated by the surviving nails.[21]

Among a variety of grave-goods some have a coin in the mouth to pay the fee of Charon the ferryman, one child with a first brass of Vespasian. Pottery is common, in one instance in the pre-Roman fashion of pieces from a broken pot placed around the head, a practice found at War Ditches.[22] Another burial had a box, with S-shaped fastenings and a hinge of iron, which contained five pots and had been placed in a hole beneath where the body was laid. A curious collection was found in a hole made in the side of another grave, comprising a bronze cylinder, a phallic bronze pendant, and an iron ring and ferrule. If the cylinder was the sheath of a wooden sceptre, from which the pendant was suspended, the deceased may have been a religious official. Other goods included armlets of bronze and shale and bronze brooches. One body had grains of charcoal scattered by the right leg, an association found also at Camerton (Som.)[23] but remaining a mystery, while finds of nails at the head, feet, and pelvis have been interpreted as remains of a bier.

[16] See Plate XVA. Neville, in *Arch. Jnl.* xi. 207, 212; cf. Babington, *Ancient Cambs.* 31 (Fulbourn); *Proc. Soc. Antiq.* 2nd ser. iii (1867), 36, 77 (Cantelupe Farm); Frend, in *Proc. C.A.S.* xlix. 13–23. (Arbury Road); *Proc. C.A.S.* xxix (1928), 109–10 (Linton).

[17] See p. 84 n. 18. [18] *Roman Fenland*, 210.

[19] Fox and Lethbridge, in *Proc. C.A.S.* xxvii. 53 (Guilden Morden); Babington, *Ancient Cambs.* 62 (Limlow Hill); Hughes, in *Proc. C.A.S.* x. 240–1 (Cambridge); Hughes and A. Macalister, in *Proc. C.A.S.* viii (1895), 317–18; cf. Fox, *Arch. Camb. Region*, 190; Lethbridge, in *Proc. C.A.S.* xxxix (1940), p. xiii; xl (1944), p. xi; Leth-

bridge, ibid. xlii. 117–27 (War Ditches).

[20] Browne, in *Proc. C.A.S.* lxv (1), 34–5, with refs. (Dam Hill); H. Hurwell, ibid. x (1904), 496 (Hauxton mill); Babington, *Ancient Cambs.* 62 (Limlow Hill).

[21] Fox and Lethbridge, in *Proc. C.A.S.* xxvii. 49–71; Jeffries, in *J.R.S.* lix. 223. Another wooden coffin is known at Arbury Road Site II (period I) preceding the masonry building, where an adult male had been buried wearing his sandals: Alexander, Excavation Rep. 1967, 12.

[22] Walker, in *Proc. C.A.S.* xii (1908), 270.

[23] Lethbridge, in *Proc. C.A.S.* xxxvi. 119.

There were examples of decapitated inhumations: in one the head of a woman, along with some vertebrae, had been struck off after death and placed at the feet, and in another the head was placed in the lap, a practice attested for laying the ghost of a witch. A charred inhumation in a burnt coffin, in which the headless body had been buried face downwards, may represent an unsuccessful attempt at cremation. Not all burials were carefully prepared: in one part of the site several bodies were dumped in a large trench apparently without ceremony. Both inhumations and cremations probably had grave markers probably in wood with painted epitaphs. Some markers had evidently been removed while the cemetery was in use, from the evidence of cremations and inhumations disturbed by other inhumations.

The best example of a small burial plot, probably belonging to a single family, lies alongside the road running north-east out of Cambridge at Arbury Road and may have been closely associated with the near-by Roman settlement. The sequence of burials began in the late 3rd century, and the continuity of later burial, together with overcrowding of the front teeth in several skeletons, suggests that the inhumations lying in an area marked off from the other burials, both inhumation and cremation, were those of people closely related.[24] Among three phases of burial, the first comprised four male inhumations, two of which were in wooden coffins, one containing a small glass jug and a colour-coated bowl of the late 3rd or 4th century. In later phases these burials were disturbed in a fashion which suggests scant respect. In the second phase a woman of 40 to 55 years was buried in a textile shroud in a coffin of Barnack stone lined with lead.[25] The coffin was partly covered by the mausoleum of the third phase, a rectangular structure in chalk (4·4 by 3·2 metres internally) which probably had a tiled roof, and which contained the body of a male (30–45 years) in a lead-lined coffin of Barnack stone, where the 1·5 metre coffin had been deliberately broken to allow insertion of the 1·9 metre lining. Between coffin and lining were fragments of a thin glass vessel. The skull and jaw-bone of a pony may have been deposited with the burial.[26]

Burials in two covered coffins in Barnack stone, with the standard trapezoidal form, were found close together at Gravel Hill Farm, in the burial ground north-west of Cambridge. The larger contained a male skeleton which had been disarranged through water entering the coffin, which had already once been broken and mended with iron clamps. The smaller, which measured externally 2·00 metres long, 0·35 metre high, 0·6 metre wide, and along with the 0·1 metre thick cover weighed about 800 kg., contained a female skeleton. Although neither coffin contained grave-goods, a cache near the female burial and probably associated with it consisted of four glass bottles, a colour-coated beaker probably of the 4th century, a jet armlet, two jet pins, a bone pin, a fragmentary bronze vessel, and a dish in coarse ware.[27]

What has reasonably been interpreted as the remains of a family burial plot at Linton (TL 557469) included three children and two females. One child was accompanied by a dish, and another had an assortment of trinkets, including five bronze bracelets, three penannular and two with terminals in the form of snakes' heads. The larger of the

---

[24] Fell, in *Proc. C.A.S.* xlix. 13–23.

[25] Both the lining and the skeleton were found in the coffin the wrong way round. It has been suggested that after the coffin was deposited the body and the lining were turned round in order to orientate the body correctly: Liversidge, *Britain in the Roman Empire*, 478.

[26] Another mausoleum may have existed at Litlington, where a rectangular stone structure (8·45 by 6·8 metres) parallel to the cemetery wall had two external buttresses and contained a coffin burial of a young person: Kempe, in *Archaeologia*, xxvi. 374. A good parallel occurs at Lulling-

stone (Kent): Greenfield, in *J.R.S.* xlix. 132 and plate XVIII (1–3).

[27] Babington, in Proc. *C.A.S.* ii. 289–92. A coffin burial, probably associated with others, was found in 1942 at Bourn airfield: Camb. Mus. The stone coffin with rounded head found in 1820 at the clay-pits NE. of Cambridge castle is probably Roman: R.C.H.M. *City of Camb.* i. 1. The coffin found at Cambridge by the monks of Ely may have been another Roman burial: *Bede's Eccl. Hist.* ed. Colgrave and Mynors, 394–5.

last had three smaller bronze rings strung on it, one of which was probably a penannular ear-ring and another a finger-ring. There was also a necklace of 148 jet beads, mainly of cylinder shapes of various lengths and with one or more incised grooves. Two beads were shaped like dentalium shells and another was rectangular and faceted. Those three and one of the cylindrical beads were of a different shade from the rest and more worn, perhaps re-used from an older necklace. Between the thighs were half of a shale armlet and the neck of a glass bottle, while at the right femur was a pottery jar and at the right ankle a smashed ('killed') pot. A single nail and traces of charcoal were also found.[28]

What has been published as a Roman burial from Grange Road, Cambridge, may represent a conflation of the goods from separate Roman and Saxon burials. The male burial is held to have been accompanied by a jug, a bone pin, a bronze cloak- or dress-fastener, an iron spearhead, and a 'scale of Roman armour'.[29]

Examples are recorded of the common Roman practice of burying infants beneath the floors of dwellings, from Castle Hill, Cambridge, and from Norwood, March (TL 418994), where the skeleton of a premature baby was found beneath the floor of a hut.[30]

The practice of burial in a mound may have been introduced to the area from the Low Countries or may have been a continuance of local tradition in a Romanized form. Burial mounds allegedly Roman have shown no discernible significance in their local distribution. None has been properly excavated, and some which are probably Bronze Age have been designated as Roman because of associated finds.[31] A curious barrow burial of the Roman period has been excavated at Lord's Bridge, Hey Hill (TL 394544), which was 14·5 metres long, 7·5 wide, and 2·6 high, with the long axis aligned SSW. by NNE. and built of deposits of gravel and gault, yellow sand, and sandy earth, into which a secondary inhumation was inserted. The primary burial had been placed in a pit dug in the natural gravel at the centre of the mound, the body in a lidless coffin of Barnack ragstone (2·2 metres long, 0·45 deep) of the usual trapezoid shape (0·6 metre wide at one end, 0·45 at the other, chiselled out to a thickness of 0·15 metre). The coffin was covered with gault and stones after the insertion of a female whose bones were found in the correct positions, although only the tibia and fibula were articulated. The body may have been partly dismembered, perhaps devoid of flesh as the result of exposure on a pyre, though a more unpleasant fate might be inferred. The burial was accompanied by two bone hairpins, the bones of a cock and a goose, the tooth of a sheep or goat, and the tooth of a pig, while fragments of a pot were laid around the sides of the coffin at the head end, and outside, just touching the feet end, were 27 hobnails. The date of the burial is not known, but is not likely to be earlier than the 3rd century and is more likely the 4th.[32] The destruction of a barrow at Limlow Hill, Litlington, revealed the mound to be 5·5 metres high with a diameter of 12·75 metres, built from layers of earth and chalk, and encircled by a ditch and bank. At the middle was a rectangular flint-filled pit 1·3 metres long, although no trace of a burial was noted.[33]

[28] See Plate XIB. Lethbridge, in *Proc. C.A.S.* xxxvii (1937), 68–71. No mausoleum appears to have existed there.

[29] Walker, in *Proc. C.A.S.* xvi (1912), 122–32.

[30] *Roman Fenland*, 220.

[31] Fox, *Arch. Camb. Region*, 191–200. On links with the Low Countries see Dunning and Jessup, in *Antiquity*, x. 37–53; and on Bronze Age barrows see R.C.H.M. *Cambs.* ii, p. xxxi. In the other direction the Moulton Hills at Bourn are now thought to be later than the Norman Conquest: R.C.H.M. *Cambs.* i. 27 (no. 43); they incorporate earlier refuse, and were once regarded as Roman: Walker, in *Proc. C.A.S.* xv. 166–77.

[32] Walker, in *Proc. C.A.S.* xii. 273 sqq.; cf. R.C.H.M. *Cambs.* i. 17 (no. 26).

[33] Hughes, in *Proc. C.A.S.* vi (1891), 395–6. Later excavations sectioned the ditch of a rectangular enclosure 64 metres wide associated with the barrow. The flat-bottomed ditch was 7·5 metres wide and 2 metres deep on the W., and 6·5 metres and 1·7 metres on the E. It was dated by pottery of the late 2nd century, and material from the ditch was thought to be the source of the mound. Another rectangular enclosure was noted further S. and the entire complex was contained within an incomplete Iron Age hill fort: Clark, in *Proc. C.A.S.* xxxviii. 171–5; *Proc. Prehist. Soc. E. Anglia*, ii (1936), 101–2.

Little else is known of the Roman barrows in the area. The inhumation in a stone coffin near Vallance Farm, Ickleton (TL 482418), was under a mound. A possible barrow of Roman date at Mill Way, Swavesey (TL 355691), has yielded fragments of a quern and some pottery. The conical mound at Hildersham (TL 544489), once with a diameter of 58 metres but now demolished, was found to contain a cremation burial, as did a possible Roman barrow at Linton Heath (TL 583486). The levelled remains of Deadman's Hill, Barton (TL 414558), contained Roman material, and a mound near Howe House is reported to have contained Roman coins, perhaps a burial monument alongside the Godmanchester road. A barrow presumed to be Roman at Alpha Road, Trumpington (TL 447553), lay originally within a square ditched enclosure, recalling that at Limlow Hill described above.[34] Several mounds have been assigned to the Roman period on topographical grounds notably at Comberton, Low Hill in Fen Drayton (TL 337693, 24·3 metres diam. and 1·2 high), Shudy Camps (approx. TL 62654502), Fulbourn Valley Farm, between Balsham and Worsted Lodge, and the four at Wilburton.[35]

Barrow burials are rare and were perhaps wholly restricted to the wealthiest families, who may have been settlers from outside the province. Their settlement was extensive if all the barrows described were indeed Roman. The earliest in the county dates to the 2nd century, although similar burials elsewhere are earlier, and the tradition persisted into the late Roman period if the dating of the coffins is reliable.

[34] Material in Camb. Mus. (Ickleton); Fox, *Arch. Camb. Region*, 149 (Trumpington), 195–6 (Hildersham and Linton), 298 (Swavesey); Neville, in *Arch. Jnl.* xi. 95 (Linton); *Proc. C.A.S.* xiv (1910), 53; cf. D. and S. Lysons, *Magna Britannia*, ii, *Cambs.* 44; Babington, *Ancient Cambs.* 35 (Barton); R.C.H.M. *City of Camb.* i. 4 (no. 6); cf. Camb. Univ. Libr., MS. d. 889. 22, 11–12 (Trumpington).

[35] Fox, *Arch. Camb. Region*, 198; for Fulbourn cf. Neville, in *Arch. Jnl.* xi. 212. The well preserved bronze jugs and glass from Hauxton mill may have come from barrow burials: cf. Liversidge, in *Proc. C.A.S.* li. 7–17.

INDEX